FREE
TO BE
Me

BREAK THROUGH THE LIES
—— TO UNCOVER THE ——
TRUE YOU

By
Natasha Hazlett
with
24 Unstoppable Women of Influence

Soul Food
PUBLISHING

ISBN: 978-0-9994735-7-3

Soul Food Publishing, Franklin, Tennessee

Author Photograph: Amy Allmand Photography

Cover Design: WildEagle Studio

*In loving memory of Vanessa Bryson,
a true Unstoppable Influencer.*

*Her unshakable faith in God, unstoppable
spirit, humor, and inspiring words will live
in our hearts forever.*

CONTENTS

A Note From the Author vii

Introduction xi

Chapter 1: The Power of Belief 1

Chapter 2: How to Eliminate Limiting Beliefs 5

Chapter 3: From Broken to Whole
by Andrea Dell 19

Chapter 4: From Alone to Supported
by Annette Steiger 29

Chapter 5: From Weak to Strong
by Martha L. Brognard 39

Chapter 6: From Controlling to Trusting
by Christine Hoy 49

Chapter 7: From Lost to Found
by Christine L. Stallard 59

Chapter 8: From Scared to Confident
by Colleen Rekers 69

Chapter 9: From Scared to Brave
by Donna Connor 79

Chapter 10: From Not Enough to a Gift
by Ellie West 89

Chapter 11: From Deficient to Proficient
by Karen Kahn 97

Chapter 12: From Total Train Wreck to Divinely Aligned
by Lisa Cain 107

Chapter 13: From Bossy to Decisive
by Maria DeLorenzis Reyes 115

Chapter 14: From Hidden to Seen
by May Simpson. 125

Chapter 15: From Failure to Infinite Potential
by Misty Lyon. 135

Chapter 16: From Indecisive to Confident
by Ruth Reynolds Smith 143

Chapter 17: From I Should to I Could
by Becky Wallery 153

Chapter 18: From Restrained to Unleashed
by Cassandra Lennox 163

Chapter 19: From Timid to Bold
by Erin Gardiner. 173

Chapter 20: From I Can't to I Can
by Gina Faust 183

Chapter 21: From Divorced to Whole
by Heather Romanski 193

Chapter 22: From Too Sensitive to Gifted Empath
by Kristin Oakley 201

Chapter 23: From Worthless to Worthy
by Oneisis Frias. 211

Chapter 24: From Abandoned to Restored
by Marilyn Hart 221

Chapter 25: From Problem to Wonderfully Made
by Vanessa Bryson 231

Chapter 26: From Unloved to Loved
by Tricia Speas 239

Chapter 27: Now, It's Your Turn 247

References 293

A NOTE FROM THE AUTHOR

For well over a decade, I've been blessed to coach women around the world to get the clarity, confidence, and strategies they need to find and fulfill their life's callings.

For the past few years, though, I've noticed an alarming trend: an increase in overwhelm and confusion and a loss of identity. Many people are struggling to find the clarity and truth about who they are. You may very well be one of them. If so, I'm thrilled you picked up this book.

If you're someone who looks in the mirror and doesn't recognize the person staring back at you...or worse, if you don't like the person staring back at you...

If you've entered a new season of life, and you're struggling with your identity...

If you're a "people pleaser" by nature, like me, you may be feeling lost because you've spent your whole life living for the approval of others...

Maybe past wounds have left you unable to confidently answer the question, "Who am I?"

If any of this sounds familiar, you're not alone. So many of us have spent years bound by the chains of limitation in our own minds. They've prevented us from living our best lives and reaching our God-given potential.

The great news is, we really don't have to live this way!

In *Free To Be Me*, you'll discover how people just like you have freed themselves from common limiting beliefs and how you can do the same!

Before you dive in, and because I'm a lawyer, I want to make a quick disclaimer:

I, along with many of the co-authors of this book, am a woman of faith. If the mention of God or scripture makes you a bit uneasy, I offer you a couple of options…

A. Come and stay a while with an open mind, and take what resonates with you.

B. Close the book, and ultimately close your mind to a potentially life-altering perspective.

You certainly don't need to be a Christian to benefit from this book. That said, if you are a Believer, I invite you to pray on what you read and discern what God may be revealing to you about your own personal chains of limitation that have been holding you back from answering God's callings for your life.

I'm confident that you will connect deeply with many of the inspiring, brave, and vulnerable women who have contributed to this book. Each chapter has a brief summary at the end filled with Key Takeaways, along with specific Free Yourself activities to help you put the inspiration into action!

I'm honored to have you on this journey with us. It's no accident that you're reading this book. You're here on purpose and for a purpose. Your freedom awaits. I can't wait to hear your breakthrough story!

Natasha N. Hazlett
Franklin, Tennessee

INTRODUCTION

I remember the day so clearly…

I was sitting in a marketing event, surrounded by 1,500 entrepreneurs. Everyone was energized, pumped up, and dreaming big.

I, on the other hand, was sad and insecure.

My Inner Critic told me that I was the least successful person in that room…and the most unattractive. I didn't belong there, and it was just a matter of time before someone called me out on it.

Despite my fears and feelings of unworthiness, I forced myself to walk through the doors of that conference every morning for three days. And every morning, my cheeks were hot with insecurity. I felt like the odd girl out.

Every day, my Inner Critic suggested that I just leave, that no one would miss me if I was gone. Yet something within told me to keep pushing through and continue listening because there was something specifically for me at that conference—I just hadn't gotten it yet.

Then Marcus Lemonis walked onto the stage. After sharing a vulnerable story about his childhood, he asked the audience:

"What's something that you haven't told ANYBODY, and how does it affect your business?"

The answer dropped on my heart immediately.

I hate myself.

It was shocking and sad, but very true.

No one knew that I hated myself. When I looked in the mirror, I couldn't stand the woman staring back at me!

I was 210 pounds on a 5' 5" frame, stats that landed me in the "clinically obese" category. I had been on weight-loss pills or some form of diet since I was 12 years old.

I had hair that would never style quite right, thanks to its tendency to frizz up at the slightest bit of humidity.

I was top-heavy, a feature far too many weren't shy about commenting on, insisting it was a blessing. I felt otherwise: it made me painfully insecure.

The cherry on top? I had strabismus.

Never heard of it? Neither did I until I was 42 because most people called it by the name that stung so deeply my entire life: lazy eye. Some particularly cruel guys in college called it a "crazy eye."

No wonder I never felt beautiful on the outside…or the inside, for that matter.

Others viewed me as a successful entrepreneur. After all, the business my husband and I had started back in 2010 had crossed the five-year mark, generated multiple six figures annually, and enabled me to retire from my full-time law practice at the age of 33.

Yet I could never "see" myself as accomplished. I saw only what others had achieved that I had not. Which meant that I always felt like I never quite measured up. The fact that we had "just" a six-figure business while others had crossed the highly coveted million-dollar mark made me feel…well, like a loser.

With those beliefs, it was no surprise that when I looked in the mirror, I hated the person staring back at me. My Inner Critic told me I was "fat, ugly, lazy, and a loser who would never measure up."

Obviously, I kept that indictment to myself for years.

But to answer Marcus's question "How did that affect our business?" It affected everything!

Just a couple of weeks before the conference, I had told my husband that I wanted to quit our business and go back to practicing law. I didn't want to inspire anyone. I had no desire to be onstage. I was a wreck—physically, spiritually, mentally, and emotionally. I felt like I would never achieve the levels of success that others had, so my Inner Critic convinced me that I should just quit our business.

Yet in spite of my desire to quit, I forced myself to attend that conference, which was just a couple of weeks after my meltdown.

So there I sat, surrounded by strangers, with the painful realization that I hated myself. OUCH.

Then something miraculous happened—a true God moment. For the first time in my life, I had a desire to LOVE myself. I didn't have a clue *how* I could do it, or *if* I could even do it. But I was willing to try.

As if on cue, I had another revelation: the fat on my body was a physical manifestation of my hatred for myself. Once I recognized it for what it was, I wanted that fat gone—immediately.

I tell the whole story in my first book, *Unstoppable Influence: Be You. Be Fearless. Transform Lives.* But to fast-forward a bit, I lost 55 pounds in five and a half months. My weight-loss journey put me on the path to finding out who I really was and to begin loving myself, flaws and all.

As I sat on the plane heading home from the conference, I began a process I later dubbed Unbecoming™. It's based on this quote:

> "*Maybe the journey isn't so much about becoming someone. Maybe it's about unbecoming everything that isn't really you, so you can be who you were meant to be in the first place.*"

I needed to not only uncover the Truth about who I am but also to free myself from the lies that I, and others, had spoken over me. I knew that this was the *only* way that I could truly love myself.

The late motivational speaker Sean Stephenson told the audience at an event I attended that he truly loved himself. It was a bold statement considering Sean was three feet tall, had brittle bones due to osteogenesis imperfecta, and had used a wheelchair his entire life. He had every reason to feel insecure, yet this man boldly proclaimed to thousands of people that he loved himself, and I believed him.

Sean explained that we must love ourselves so that we can truly love others. At the time, I thought the whole concept was kinda hokey because I was convinced that "self-love" was a bunch of esoteric nonsense. I was wrong.

I discovered that when you hate yourself, it's hard to love others fully. And when your Inner Critic is constantly tearing you down, it's difficult to inspire and positively influence others. Without self-acceptance and self-love, you'll beat yourself up as you journey through life.

That's no way to live. I should know because I did it for at least 30 years.

My Unbecoming journey revealed just how much the words spoken to and about me had been holding me back from achieving God's callings and purpose for my life.

It was as if I was chained up by my beliefs about who I was and what I was capable of doing in this world. I was being held captive by a force that wanted nothing more than to silence and sideline me.

Fortunately, that's not the end of my story. It's just the beginning.

Once I saw the chains of my limiting beliefs and identified the culprit behind them, I set my sights on freedom from the lies and limitations...and I succeeded. I can unequivocally say that I feel truly free to be the woman God made me to be.

I'm no longer restrained by the limiting beliefs that held me back for so long.

I now look in the mirror and LOVE the woman staring back at me (even though I'm currently not at my ideal weight, and I have yet to find a frizz-free hair product that actually works).

I now feel free to share my most vulnerable feelings without the fear of what others may think. In fact, my first book, *Unstoppable Influence*, shared a host of stories that "old Natasha" would never have dared utter aloud to anyone, much less on a public stage.

Then I took things a step further. Not only did I publish my book, we've sold over 18,000 copies to date! I even went on TV and spoke openly to thousands of people about some of my most vulnerable feelings, including showing a video I had recorded of my own personal rock-bottom moment.

Unstoppable Influence ultimately served as a launchpad for a more in-depth 21-day challenge experience where I empower thousands of women to go through their own Unbecoming process and free themselves from their chains of limitation. By Unbecoming everything they aren't, our clients begin seeing their worth, ultimately becoming more confident in their own skin.

Unstoppable Influence challenges have also led countless women to finally uncover their callings, write the books that have been on their hearts, start their own coaching practices, share their vulnerable stories of triumph over tragedy onstage, or start the businesses of their dreams.

Once we're free to be ourselves, the possibilities are truly endless.

Right now, you may feel like I did years ago in that conference room surrounded by thousands of strangers.

You may feel worthless, unlovable, broken, unattractive, or not enough.

You may believe that you're too smart, undereducated, too loud, too quiet, too [you name it].

The truth is, you are a divine masterpiece and an incredible gift to this world. You have been reverently and lovingly designed by your Creator on purpose and for an important purpose. You were literally made for such a time as this.

The world needs the authentic you.

Not the person you think others want you to be.

Not the person the media says you should be.

Not even the person your family thinks you should be.

If you're ready to free yourself from your past and the lies spoken to and about you and uncover the radiant truth about who you truly are, then turn the page…because your freedom awaits!

CHAPTER 1

THE POWER OF BELIEF

As I embarked on my own journey of Unbecoming, I began to read and listen to every personal development book and training I could get my hands on. Along the way, I discovered the concept of limiting beliefs and the impact they can have on our lives. What I learned was transformational.

All our beliefs are rooted deeply within our subconscious mind. Have you ever pulled into the parking lot of a store you frequently shop at, then thought to yourself, *How did I get here?! I don't remember stopping at a red light or making the left turn!*

The answer is likely yes. (I've asked audiences this question before, so I know it's not just me!)

So how did you get to the store safely? Were you paying attention? The answer is yes because your subconscious mind was in action.

When you drive a route hundreds of times, you don't consciously think about putting on the brakes or pushing the accelerator each and every time. You don't have to consciously think about making the turns or stopping at red lights. You just do it.

Our subconscious mind is a driving force in our life. The beliefs stored there impact every facet of our day-to-day existence. If you look around at your current circumstances, chances are they're the direct or indirect results of subconscious beliefs you have about yourself.

Here's why—beliefs inform your decisions. Your decisions dictate your action (or inaction), and typically it's your action (or inaction) that determines the results you experience.

So if you don't like the results you're getting in life and you want to change them, the best place to start is by examining your beliefs.

Let me give you a real-world example.

Sarah is a certified life coach. She has built her own coaching practice and is at the point where she wants to grow her business beyond just word-of-mouth clients, so she hires a well-respected business coach.

Her business coach notices that Sarah isn't on social media and suggests that she start regularly posting content of value related to her business.

But Sarah *doesn't take action* on her coach's advice because she *decided* that "social media isn't her thing." *As a result,* her business doesn't grow.

Sarah sees other participants in the program generating more clients and making more money. She starts feeling ashamed and wonders what's wrong with her business. Why isn't it growing like everyone else's?

Her Inner Critic suggests that she's "just not a good enough life coach," and that's why her business isn't growing. Soon Sarah becomes frustrated and resentful, which only makes her not want to market her coaching practice.

As Sarah begins going through one of the first steps of the Unbecoming process, she remembers that when she was younger, her parents frequently told her to "be quiet," that she was being "way too loud," and that "children are to be seen not heard."

Up until that point, she'd forgotten those words. But those repeated comments from her parents had imprinted within Sarah's subconscious mind a belief that she didn't have anything valuable to say.

It's no wonder that every time Sarah started to write a post, her Inner Critic jeered, "What's the point in posting? No one wants to listen to you." Or, "You just need to keep scrolling—you don't have anything valuable to say."

In this example, Sarah's result (her business being stagnant) is due to her own INACTION, which was a result of her DECISION that "social media isn't her thing," which was fueled by a BELIEF that she didn't have anything valuable to say.

See how that works?

If you want to change your results, you must change your actions. If you want to change your actions, you'll need to first change your beliefs!

CHAPTER 2

HOW TO ELIMINATE LIMITING BELIEFS

If the results we experience in life are the by-product of our beliefs, then where do those beliefs come from?

All beliefs begin as thoughts. Napoleon Hill, in the timeless classic *Think and Grow Rich*, says: "Thoughts are things, and powerful things at that..."

Thoughts are extremely powerful because they're the precursors to all beliefs.

When our mind is flooded with toxic, self-sabotaging thoughts, limited and disempowering beliefs are formed. Those beliefs lead us to take actions, or maintain the status quo, which may prevent us from experiencing the results we desire and ultimately may keep us from fulfilling our calling and purpose.

What *if* there were a way to keep those limiting beliefs from being formed? That would be a game-changer, right?

Fortunately, there *are* ways to prevent these types of beliefs from being formed! Yes, these methods *can* work for you–even if you're like I was years ago, constantly battling one negative thought after another.

There are also ways to rewire your brain to eliminate unhelpful beliefs from your subconscious mind. But before I give you some proven ways to neutralize negative thoughts, I want to share a powerful visualization strategy.

The Thought Seed

For the purposes of taking control of a thought, visualize it as a little seed in your hand. If you don't do anything with the seed, it can't grow into anything. However, if you plant the seed, water it, and put it in the sunlight, it will begin to take root in the soil and ultimately grow.

A thought entering your mind is nothing more than a seed. Unless you do something with it by coming into agreement with or adopting that thought, nothing can happen. The thought can't take root, so a limiting belief won't grow from it.

A limiting belief is essentially a story we tell ourselves about who we are or what we're capable of that holds us back from becoming who we are meant to be. Limiting beliefs prevent us from reaching our full potential.

I know what you're probably thinking right now: *What about limiting beliefs that have already taken root?*

Great news! You have the power to consciously decide to come out of agreement with *any* limiting belief whenever you want.

I learned about the concept of agreements from a counselor and author named John Eldredge. Here's how John defines it in his book *Walking with God*.

> By agreements, I mean those subtle convictions we come to, assent to, give way to, or are raised to assume are true. It happens down deep in our souls where our real beliefs about life are formed. Something or someone whispers to us "Life is never going to turn out the way you'd hoped," or "Nobody's going to come through," or God has forsaken you." And something in us responds, "That's true." We make an agreement with it and a conviction is formed.

How many agreements have you made over the years about who you are and what you're capable of doing?

As I reflected on my own life, I realized that I had made countless agreements (both consciously and unconsciously) that resulted in some very self-sabotaging, limiting beliefs. These "invisible" convictions had very real effects on my life and my business.

For example, in 2016, I was so convinced that I was un-attractive and not good enough to be truly successful in our business (which required me to be on camera and onstage), I nearly walked away from our business!

Had I actually quit, my first book, *Unstoppable Influence,* never would have been written. And without the book, we would never have built a multiple-seven-figure brand that has transformed thousands of lives!

Numerous women have shared that my book and the 21-Day Challenge literally saved them from ending their own lives. Others have said that it mended their marriage and did more to help them than years of therapy! Countless women have said that my book brought them back to God.

Had I believed the lies, I wouldn't have been able to impact the lives of those who needed my gifts and my light. In short, the Enemy's lies nearly destroyed my business and starved thousands of women of their breakthroughs.

Thanks to divine intervention at that conference in 2016, I uncovered the lies I'd been believing and discovered the Truth about who I am and what I'm capable of doing. When I broke the agreements relating to my appearance and my potential, life changed dramatically.

Make no mistake, friend—there is a battle for your mind...a spiritual one.

God wants to prosper you, to give you hope and a future. He has good plans for your life. The Enemy comes to steal, kill, and destroy. He wants to sideline you. He doesn't want you to fulfill your callings or to live out your God-given purpose.

So we have to be on guard. We need to know how to protect our minds from allowing toxic thoughts to turn into self-sabotaging, limiting beliefs.

The great news is you CAN absolutely protect your mind from this assault. I'll break this process down into two parts: how to handle a thought and how to break an existing agreement.

How to Handle a Negative Thought

First, when a negative thought comes into your mind, bring awareness to it. Visualize it as a little seed in your hand.

Next, identify it as either a good or bad seed. Is this a seed that if planted will serve you well? Is it positive, empowering, uplifting?

If the answer is yes, then go ahead and come into agreement with that thought. Adopt it. Allow it to enter your mind and become a part of who you are.

If, upon examination, you determine that the thought is a bad seed—for example, an accusation like "I always mess things up" or "I'm not smart"—then you'll want to renounce that thought. Refuse to come into agreement with it!

I'll say softly out loud or in my mind things like...

"Nice try, but no."

"That's a lie. I reject it!"

There aren't any magic words. It's simply the intention behind the words you think or speak in relation to the thought. Make sure you're actively deciding to disregard and discard the negative thought.

Finally, if it's a negative thought or accusation, replace it with the Truth.

As a Christian, I turn to the Word of God, which is filled with Truth about who I am, who God is, and God's promises for me. As it says in John 8:32, when we know the Truth, we are set free.

How to Handle Existing Limiting Beliefs

If you're like most people, you have an extensive list of limiting or self-sabotaging beliefs. The good news is that you can totally rewire your brain.

Dr. Caroline Leaf, a cognitive neuroscientist, has been studying the brain for over 30 years. She and others have found that the mind and brain are **neuroplastic,** meaning they can change.

According to Dr. Leaf, "Everything we do begins with a thought. **If we want to change anything in our lives, we first have to change our thinking, which means changing our mind!**" (Emphasis mine.)

There are numerous ways to rewire your brain with respect to limiting beliefs.

I have personally experienced transformational results with neuro-linguistic programming (NLP) and hypnotherapy. Both of these methods can also be helpful because they work on the root cause of the beliefs—your subconscious mind. These methods are particularly helpful for deeply rooted, long-standing beliefs.

Additionally, I use the strategy of breaking agreements, like what we did with the bad thought seed. Remember, the key to coming out of agreement with an existing limiting belief, is first **becoming aware** of it.

Awareness is part of the Unbecoming process I teach in *Unstoppable Influence* and in our Unstoppable Influence challenge. One of the exercises I have our clients do is write out their backstories. By writing out your backstory, you'll find many limiting beliefs that have come from your past experiences.

For example, ever since a little punk called me Hairy Legs in my fifth-grade art camp, I had a limiting belief that I was ugly. Others calling me names due to my strabismus only further fueled this belief.

The Enemy and his minions preyed on my vulnerability around my appearance, so every time I was about to shoot a video or post one I'd made, my mind would be flooded with thoughts about how unattractive I was.

This agreement did not serve me well. It nearly caused me to quit my business! Had I followed through, you wouldn't be reading this book. And the thousands of women who experienced transformational breakthroughs because of me would have been deprived of their life-changing shifts.

The Apostle Paul, in 2 Corinthians 10:5 (NIV) says: "[T]ake captive every thought to make it obedient to Christ."

Taking your thoughts captive simply means gaining control over what you think about yourself and life. You're in the driver's seat! Spiritually, it's important to remember that the Enemy can't control your thoughts; he can merely suggest them. You're in control of what happens next.

After you bring awareness to the past limiting belief, the next step is to simply renounce it. I prefer to do this out loud because of the power of the spoken word.

You can simply say: "I renounce the belief that I am [*insert limiting belief*]!"

Christians should consider renouncing the belief in the name of Jesus.

That's it for Step 2.

The final step is to replace the limiting belief with the Truth and evidence in support of that Truth.

For example, I replaced the lie I had repeated for decades that "I am ugly" with "I am beautiful." I supported this truth with the following evidence:

✦ God made me just the way that I am.

✦ My husband always tells me that I'm beautiful.

In the chapters that follow, you will read stories from amazing women who broke free from the lies and uncovered their true selves.

They have shared their epiphany moments in the hopes that their "aha moment" will inspire your own breakthrough!

Before you start reading their stories, I encourage you to write down some of the lies you frequently have spoken over yourself.

On the next page is a list of some common ones to get you started.

I am unworthy.

I am uncapable.

I am uneducated.

I am unlovable.

I am ugly.

I don't have the time.

I don't have what it takes.

I don't have the will-power.

I don't have the skills or talent.

I am bad at technology.

I'm too inexperienced.

I don't understand.

I always make mis-takes.

No one will like my idea.

I'll get rejected.

I'm not brave enough.

I'm not strong enough.

I'm not creative enough.

I can't do it.

I'm too old/young.

I'm too fat/skinny.

I'm too out of shape.

I'm too tired.

I'm too shy.

I'm always wrong.

I'm too bossy.

I'm a bad friend.

I'm too broken for a relationship.

I'm all alone.

I'm too quiet.

I'm too much.

I don't deserve love.

I have to be perfect.

I am not good with money.

I grew up poor, so I'll always be poor.

I'll always be in debt.

I'll never have enough money to feel secure.

I could never do that.

I'm broken.

KEY TAKEAWAYS

✦ All beliefs begin with a thought.

✦ Thoughts are like seeds—unless you come into agreement with or adopt them, they cannot become beliefs.

✦ A limiting belief is a story about who we are or what we're capable of that holds us back from reaching our potential.

✦ Our brains are neuroplastic, which means they can change. We can rewrite the "stories" we tell ourselves.

FREE YOURSELF

1. Write out your backstory. Then go back and review it to identify limiting beliefs that have stemmed from your life experiences.

2. Write down some of the lies that you frequently have spoken over yourself from the list above, or create your own list.

3. Break any unhelpful agreements using the three-step process:

   1. Identify it.

   2. Renounce it.

   3. Replace it with the Truth.

4. For stubborn, long-held limiting beliefs, consider working with a certified NLP practitioner or hypnotherapist. You can get access to a directory of them in the companion workbook, which you can download for free at DesignYourBestLife.com/gift.

CHAPTER 3

FROM BROKEN TO WHOLE

by Andrea Dell

> *I was afraid of my own power, afraid that it would threaten people, intimidate people. And it's a great sadness wishing to be less than you actually are. And it's hard to take on the world when you're constantly in a battle with yourself.*

— Nicole Kidman

I stared back at my parents, my eight-year-old mind unable to comprehend what I'd just heard. As my sisters and I sat in our living room while they delivered the news, my sense of safety instantly split wide open, leaving a painful, gaping wound I didn't understand or know how to close.

My parents' divorce is my first clear memory of feeling broken. My child's mind subconsciously reasoned that if our family had to break up, I must have caused it. Self-blame weighed on me like a boulder strapped to my back. My parents insisted it wasn't my fault, yet for reasons I still don't understand, I was determined to blame myself.

Without meaning to, I fell into a pattern of blaming myself and feeling BROKEN when "bad things" happened. When I was picked on or made fun of at school, rejected by anyone (for anything), or a circumstance didn't turn out the way I wanted, thoughts like these reinforced my brokenness:

> *If I were a better person, things would have worked out the way I expected.*
>
> *If I were a better person, people I want to spend time with would not keep rejecting me.*
>
> *If I were a better person, I would not keep screwing up and depriving myself of the life I want.*

Feeling broken every day was a miserable existence, so I tried to numb the pain by binging on TV and movies and playing loads of video games. Sometimes I resorted to food and soda, but escaping into other worlds and living vicariously through a screen were how I most often coped with my misery.

In July of 2017, things finally began to shift. I was unexpectedly let go from a long-time job. Being fired flipped a switch. I felt like a failure, and I was tired of it. At the time, I couldn't have told you exactly why I felt like a failure, but I was about to find out.

In October of that year, I attended the first-ever Unstoppable Influence Summit in Boise, Idaho, where author, speaker, and celebrity hypnotist Joseph Clough took the summit audience through a process to identify what he calls "your one core issue." He explained that this is a buried belief you have about yourself that's responsible for negative symptoms like anxiety, phobias, depression, and procrastination.

At the end of his presentation, he asked us to close our eyes and "listen" internally for what came up as the root cause of all our unwanted symptoms. Immediately, one short sentence popped into my mind: *I don't trust myself.*

Hearing those words inside my own head, I felt like I'd been punched in the gut. But at the same time, it was a huge breakthrough because it explained *so* much!

For years, without realizing it, I'd let myself down over and over. I made commitments to myself that I failed to keep and betrayed myself in order to please someone else. I took on burdens that weren't mine to bear, like my parents' divorce, then blamed myself if I couldn't carry those burdens. No wonder I felt broken!

It was a pivotal moment to be sure, and you'd think this new awareness would have provided relief from my never-ending efforts to "fix myself," but it didn't. The belief that I need to be fixed was still too ingrained.

I joined the Unstoppable Influence Inner Circle that year and dove headfirst into the coaching and personal development support. I wish I could say it was because I wanted to evolve myself, but it was actually because I still thought I needed to be fixed. Leaning into personal development, I definitely grew over the next few years, but I kept hitting that same frustrating wall standing between me and feeling whole. Little did I know things were about to change...

February 16, 2022, began like any other day. I got up, and took my dog, Marlee, outside to go potty. After feeding us both and showering, I dove into my copy-writing work. At around 3:40 in the afternoon, I leashed Marlee for her afternoon walk.

I had adopted Marlee, a black-and-tan corgi/chihuahua mix with giant bat ears and the cutest face, from a family member in 2017. She loved people, other dogs, and even cats. Marlee was a gentle, happy soul and a great fit for my lifestyle.

We walked to a community park she liked. It sported a poop station with dog-waste bags and lots of grass. We'd visited this park dozens of times. That day, we encountered an unfamiliar man and unrestrained dog.

As soon as the dog spotted Marlee, it made a beeline for her and, despite my efforts to prevent the encounter, viciously attacked her. The man managed to pull the dog off before it could kill her, but the damage was done. Marlee was terrified and gravely injured.

I rushed her to two different veterinary clinics, where I was told that she would need surgery costing as much as $10,200 (which didn't include follow-up care) to determine whether she could even BE saved. Worse, there was no certainty around her quality of life afterward. But this surgery was her only chance at survival.

Even with such grim news, I came very close to saying yes to the surgery. But ultimately, rather than put Marlee through a grueling surgery that might not actually save her and risk a terrible quality of life afterwards, I made the heart-wrenching decision to have little Marlee put to sleep.

The whole thing left me completely wrecked. Grief over losing her was bad enough, but it was the guilt over choosing to walk her on that day, at that time, then opting for euthanasia over an intense surgery with an uncertain outcome that ripped me apart.

Combined with the trauma of seeing and hearing her attacked, I collapsed to a form of rock bottom I didn't recall ever experiencing before. Replays of Marlee's attack forced their way into my mind all day and into the night, terrorizing me almost as intensely as the attack itself.

Over the next few months, my body reacted to the trauma in ways I didn't expect. My capacity to handle physical or emotional stress dropped to zilch overnight. I stopped consuming caffeine for two weeks, figuring my body didn't need the stimulation. But when I reintroduced it, I experienced a caffeine-amplified panic attack, which left my body even more of a wreck.

Scared to be alone, I stayed with my aunt and uncle for a few days. At my request, my aunt even took me to the emergency room to get checked out. Due to how strangely my body was reacting to Marlee's attack, I thought I might be in the throes of a heart attack. (I wasn't, thank goodness.)

Those first few months after Marlee's attack were incredibly unpredictable, with random panic attacks hitting as I walked upstairs, stepped outside to collect my mail, or even when I simply drove down the highway.

To make sense of what my body was doing, I dove into studying trauma. A cousin of mine with more trauma experience shared resources that really helped. I also explored various emotional and physical healing modalities and took supplements to support healing. All seemed to improve my situation, and as more time passed, things finally began to turn around. I went from feeling panicked just walking to my mailbox to walking five miles or more at a time. The panic attacks got further and further apart. I don't even remember the last time I had one. There's more healing to be done, but things have dramatically improved.

Marlee's unexpected attack, and subsequent healing journey, left me with a most unexpected gift, in that I spent so much of 2022 feeling broken that I *finally* grew tired of that label.

I have accepted that I don't need to keep trying to fix myself because I am NOT broken. I may have some unhelpful layers left to shed, but underneath them, I am WHOLE. And what's more, I CAN trust myself.

Difficult life experiences often leave us feeling shattered, especially when we aren't expecting them. As you pick up the pieces of who you were before these experiences, remember that just like me, you do NOT need to be fixed.

Even if you feel broken, you aren't. Your pieces are all there, concealed under layers you've taken on out of protection, out of trying to make sense of what's happened, and out of not knowing what else to do.

Recognizing you are already a whole person, and allowing that whole person to shine through, is a journey of shedding the layers smothering your true self.

Instead of running and hiding from this journey, distracting yourself from it, or avoiding it, lean into it. Embrace the many healing resources available to you so you can speed up the journey and begin to feel whole ...and do so far more quickly than you may even believe is possible!

KEY TAKEAWAYS

✦ Feeling broken can be triggered by experiences we don't want, understand, or expect. For me, it started with my parents' divorce.

✦ I used television, movies, and video games to numb how I felt about myself.

✦ I finally grew tired of feeling broken, but it took years for me to fully reject it and begin seeing myself as simply a person on a journey, having experiences and shedding layers.

✦ Healing from the traumatic attack and loss of my dog, Marlee, is what finally resolved my belief that I was broken.

✦ I don't need to fix myself, and neither do you. We get to accept ourselves for who we are now and allow our whole, true selves to shine through!

FREE YOURSELF

1. Think of times in your life when you've felt broken. What was happening? How were you feeling? Write it all down.

2. Ask yourself the following question, and write down what comes up for you: "Why am I a whole person?" If thinking of yourself as a whole person feels too unbelievable because you still believe you're broken, use this question instead: "Why am I in the process of recognizing that I am a whole person?"

3. Reread what you've written, then read it out loud to bring a sense of wholeness.

CHAPTER 4

FROM ALONE TO SUPPORTED

by Annette Steiger

*When I awake each morning, you're still
with me.*

— **Psalm 139:18 (TPT)**

As I walked through the camp cafeteria looking for a place to sit, every table was fully occupied as far as I could see. I made my way to the very back of this winding room, still finding no place to sit. I turned to look for my friend, who had been walking behind me. Suddenly, I noticed every table was empty and I was standing completely alone, tray in hand...

I awaken. Once again, my dream leaves me standing alone at camp.

Strange. Camp was always the place where I connected with God at the deepest level and where I felt engaged, accepted, and emboldened.

Camp Crestview church camp was the highlight of my summer. From the time we hit the exit and began to climb up the winding road, my excitement rose until I caught sight of the grand mansion overlooking the Columbia River Gorge. Sitting in its isolated splendor, the Manor welcomed me back for another week of summer games, new friendships, and spiritual growth.

Most of all, it held the promise of freedom to let down my guard and be fully me, if only for a week. At camp, no one held preconceived notions of who I was or should be. It was where I could discover myself.

Chapel services were my favorite part of camp. With over a hundred campers, we sang together in worship, our voices harmonizing. The acoustics carried the sounds so beautifully that it seemed like we were singing with Heaven's choir. The ministers spoke directly to our level so we could truly grasp the meaning of their teaching. I was able to let go of the world and just be with God on the mountain.

At camp, I was fearless. I tried everything. I played baseball and did surprisingly well. I helped my team win a relay race, swimming the length of the pool holding onto a greased watermelon. I played volleyball and kept up with even the fiercest of teammates. I participated in a pool game where we all attempted the same dives as the leader (emphasis on "attempted"). I even survived being smacked with a fast-flying, water-saturated Nerf ball, which left me with a black eye. I happily competed alongside everyone for every sport and activity offered.

At camp, I was inspired and liberated to worship unrestrained, open my heart fully to God, test my athletic abilities, be bold, laugh freely, and actively participate in something bigger than me. Summer camp was my mountaintop experience where I felt accepted, equal, and fully capable. At camp, I belonged.

Most importantly, camp was the place that prepared me and instilled in me the belief that I could make an impact in the world. It was the place where I experienced intimacy with God. And I learned over the years how to stay close to Him, not just for the mountaintop.

So why in my dreams do I find myself alone at camp, of all places?

In April 2016, my life changed. Terry, my husband, was promoted to Heaven at the age of 58 after a brief battle with brain cancer. I became a widow. I was suddenly single and alone.

I began to question, *Who am I without Terry?* During our 39 years together, our lives were so entwined that without him life didn't make sense. While married, I had a strong sense of belonging. When Terry was with me or when we were apart, I belonged. He always had my back. I never felt alone. Now I suddenly felt exposed, vulnerable, and alone.

This is where the recurring dreams began. Though I knew Terry had not chosen to leave, it was as if my brain was processing this loss as abandonment.

This was the first time in all my life that I had really been alone. I had been raised in a family of five. When I graduated and moved out, I lived with roommates until I got married, and then we had a family of our own.

I began to pray in earnest.

> God, I know you are with me and in me, but right now, I am having a hard time hearing you. Please God, open my eyes, my ears, my heart, and my mind to see and hear you clearly and know you more. Search my heart, God, and see if there is anything that is an obstacle between me and you... (from Psalm 139:23-24)

God answered my prayers in three specific ways.

First, God began to remind me of specific times in my life where He had been with me.

One day I was crying alone, and God reminded me of a retreat I had attended years earlier. At the end of the first service, I was praying and began to cry uncontrollably. Then I saw a picture in my mind, and it came with the understanding of a loss I was grieving: the fact that my mom had stopped holding me when I was very young, maybe one year old. It came with a sense of importance as if it were an event from my life. It was something I didn't know or remember in my conscious mind. When raised to my awareness, I assumed that my mom's actions must have been due to her health.

The next morning, I was again praying when suddenly I felt as if I were wrapped in a thick blanket and was being held and rocked gently. I sensed God telling me, "I'm holding you now."

Next, God brought people into my pathway whose words brought comfort, insight, and healing.

One day, I met a young man from Israel. He took my hand, then very nervously said, "I feel like I am supposed to tell you that your life is not over, that you have much more life to live." Then he proceeded to tell me how they deal with death in Israel and ended with the words "release, release, release."

I didn't know what I was supposed to be releasing, I didn't know what I was hanging on to, but I knew that God had met me there that day.

Three months later, I saw an acupuncturist at my doctor's recommendation. The woman held my right wrist and said, "There is deep sadness, maybe grieving…"

I was shocked. "You can tell that from my *wrist*?" I shared my story with her, then she told me how they deal with death in China, ending with "release, release, release."

Three months later, a man stopped me in the hall at work. I didn't know him, but I had seen him in some meetings. He began to ask me questions, then he told me how they deal with death in India, and at the end of his explanation, he said "release, release, release."

Three strangers from three countries three months apart telling me to "release, release, release." With each encounter, I knew there was no coincidence that God had brought these people to me for that specific message and moment. What I didn't know yet was what I was still holding on to.

Months later, I was listening to an online church service. At the end, the pastor said, "Release what you believed your life would be in this season, and receive healing for your broken heart."

Until that moment, I hadn't known what I was holding on to, but this was so specific, I knew it was for me. My life was nothing like I had anticipated for this season.

This time, along with release was the action to *receive*. I experienced a huge shift that day.

Then, God showed me things I could let go of.

While at a stop sign one morning, I remembered something I'd said years earlier that had embarrassed me. I felt the emotion all over again and thought, *Wow! Why do I still feel the same embarrassment now as I did when it happened? It makes no sense. I'm sure I am the only person that even gave it a second thought.*

I prayed, "Father, thank you that Your grace covers me." And I let it go. It was so simple, but it completely freed me of the emotion attached to the memory.

Now each time an emotion-packed memory surfaces, I quickly pray and release it. I've realized that I had been storing things inside that I never needed to.

Throughout this journey, God also brought scriptures, songs, books, movies, and other things to guide me and to demonstrate that He loves me, He is leading me, He is watching over me, and I am not alone.

In this most difficult transition in my life, when I was feeling the most alone I had ever been, God reminded me of my roots—the place where I built my foundation on Him, where I learned to let the world fall away and hold on to God.

Now in the dream, I walk through the camp cafeteria looking for a place to sit. Every table is fully occupied as far as I can see. This time, I find a chair and take a seat at the table because I know that I belong. And I understand at the deepest core of my being that I am never alone. God is with me and He has never—and will never—leave or abandon me. He created me with intrinsic value, and because I am His daughter, He is already pleased with me.

KEY TAKEAWAYS

✦ You are never alone, even when you feel lonely. Ask God to open your eyes, ears, heart, and mind to see and hear Him and understand His love.

✦ God uses various methods when He guides us. You can find times in your life where God has guided you, provided for you, or protected you.

✦ There is life-changing value in tapping into the memories where you felt you were able to live the most authentically you.

✦ The reasons behind your limiting beliefs or trapped emotions may not matter. If they do, God will make you aware. The release of the belief or emotion and the resulting freedom are the rewards.

✦ God created you with intrinsic value, simply because you are His daughter, and He is already pleased with you. No performance needed nor hoops to jump.

FREE YOURSELF

1. Schedule regular time to get away with God: personal retreats, ladies' meetings, or any quiet place where you can get away from distractions.

2. When a thought pops into your mind that carries negative emotions, acknowledge it by asking God for assistance or another method of release.

3. List all the people in your life who love and support you. Make plans to engage with them so that they too feel loved, supported, and never alone.

CHAPTER 5

FROM WEAK TO STRONG

by Martha L. Brognard

*Own your magic, walk in your purpose, and rock
your truth!*

— Beverly Bond

I remember when the thought of becoming a law enforcement agent first crossed my mind. I was an intelligence analyst who created background products on individuals who might possibly be selling firearms to the criminal element. I would then send this information to the field for further investigation.

My boss at the time insisted that because I was already making cases for the agents, I should just join the ranks and do the investigation myself.

My thought: *True, but that's ridiculous! For heaven's sake, I am an English major with no experience in law enforcement!*

I figured that he had to be joking! But he was not. So I started to consider the opportunity.

Was I ready to arrest bad guys, conduct search warrants, and be on call 24/7? More importantly, and the singular thought that kept crossing my mind: *Was I ready to carry a gun?!*

This potential new job was exciting and intriguing, yet frightening at the same time. So I decided to discuss the possibility with the two people I trusted the most: my parents.

Needless to say, they were NOT happy with the idea. I was a young woman, only 23. While at first I had blown off the idea as ridiculous, the thought had already started to take root, and the tree began to grow.

Imagine coming to work and no two days would ever be the same!

One gun, one crime—what story would it tell?

Where would it lead me?

Whose lives could I save?

My dad ultimately thought my decision was admirable. So with his support and my desire to improve the world, I decided to take the next step and apply for the position.

I was hired, but it took six years for the department to have a spot for me.

The thought crossed my mind more than once: *Am I crazy to want to leave my current position? Could I really do this?*

In 1999, I shoved my doubts and insecurities aside and answered the call. I became a federal agent.

Was I terrified?

Did I wonder if I was strong enough?

Did I worry whether the men on the job would look down on me, intimidate me, and think I was weak?

You bet I did!

So I prepared like crazy for the training. I was determined to earn the respect of my colleagues.

Becoming a federal law enforcement agent involved a rigorous six-month training period in a small town in southern Georgia, where I would encounter every biting bug under the sun from April to September. Not to mention energy-draining heat, and worse, the perception from my colleagues that I did not belong there.

Since there were only a few women in the class, I felt pressure to prove I was one of the best. There was a two-week break in between training segments, during which I returned to my designated office in Virginia. That was my first big test.

My assignment during that time was to move all my training agent's things to the back office, large enough to house two people.

Welcome to the man's world.

Luckily there were already two desks there, but I had to move all the rest of the training agent's junk, including two filing cabinets that first had to be emptied so I could move and then refill them. Yay, me! But I did it without complaint...well, maybe a little grumbling under my breath.

I didn't complain because before I had left my former position, my boss had taken me aside and instructed me not to be "that" person—the woman who complained. He advised me that if I did complain, I would wear that label for the rest of my career.

"Nope. Not going to be me!" I vowed. Others were ready to label me as "weak," but I would show them the truth of who I was.

One time, we were shooting pistols at these things called steel poppers. These targets allowed us to practice shooting without having to manually set them back up after each shot. Instead, they just "pop" back up.

The popper I was shooting at fell over, and when I went to reach for it, it suddenly popped up—striking me on the hand and causing a severe bruise where blood collected and pooled under my skin. It was painful, but I sucked it up because I was determined to show my strength. I was no wimp!

When my instructor heard me cry out, he came over to examine my hand. "I guess you're going to make a big deal of this and want me to rush you to the health center?"

I respectfully responded, "Sir, we're in the middle of an exercise, and I would like to continue."

A look of shock crossed his face and then a half-smile. "Guess you're tougher than I thought."

This wasn't the only time I was initially labeled "weak" at work and had to prove my strength.

I wasn't always welcome on the job, and I frequently received looks of disdain. After a short stint at my first post, I was told that I was being transferred to another office. I was horrified, as I hadn't heard anything good about my new boss. He was nicknamed "10 to 2 Joe," because those were the hours you were allowed to work (that is, when he would actually be in the office).

He was an old-school, crotchety New Yorker—a hard-ass agent. A woman on the job was a joke to him, and he was ready to rake me over the coals. The first day I walked into the office, he practically growled at me,

"Yeah, I heard we were getting one of you. You can take that desk."

He assigned a man named Scott as my training agent. I was determined to prove myself, but with this trainer, it was evident that I would be doing all the work. That was fine with me—I welcomed the challenge.

What I didn't welcome were Scott's derogatory comments about the women we saw on the street. He was constantly commenting on the size of women's breasts. This went on for about a month. I put up with it because I didn't want to be "that" woman. But when he told me I had a "decent rack," that was the last straw. He was lucky I didn't smack him across the face…and that took a LOT of restraint! But I knew it wouldn't do any good. There had to be another way.

I still didn't want to be "that" person who filed complaints. So I went home that day to think about my strategy and get my head straight.

Taking this time to pause made me reflect on times in the past when others had thought I couldn't do something. There had been times that I doubted myself, but then I would conquer that doubt with determination. As I remembered times when I had been successful by drawing on my inner strength, I knew that now was the time to tap into it again.

The next morning, summoning every bit of that inner strength but feeling extremely anxious, I walked straight into 10 to 2 Joe's office and said, "I don't want to be 'that' person who files a sexual harassment complaint, but if I have to listen to Scott talk about the size of a woman's breasts one more time, I will file. Enough is enough. Get me a new training officer!"

I had a new trainer that afternoon.

Because I was a woman, I would continue to be tested, but I would rise to the occasion, determined to prevail, and eventually earn the respect of all the men in the office. I showed them the truth of who I am. I'm not weak—I am strong!

I never once filed a complaint. There were better ways to handle such situations. In the end, 10 to 2 Joe complimented me as one of the best agents in the group—that is, after a few years of proving myself. (I am pleased to say that this is no longer the case with the agency.)

Remember this: Each woman has inner strength; I do and so do you!

Women are often afraid to unleash their own strength. Only you know what you are strong enough to accomplish. Separate yourself from those who discourage you, saying, "You are weak" or, "You can't do that." Because you can!

Surround yourself with individuals who inspire you to be the best version of yourself. Trust yourself, because you are far stronger than you realize.

KEY TAKEAWAYS

✦ If an opportunity comes your way, even if it's outside of your comfort zone, leap! Empowerment, accomplishment, satisfaction, and personal growth await.

✦ Remember, perseverance pays off, and you can't let other people define who you are. Only you can do that.

✦ Fear is an emotion you can transform into determination, defiance, and strength. If you let it, fear can keep you from shining your light and making a difference in this world. Don't let fear dim your light because the world needs it.

✦ Surround yourself with individuals who inspire you to be the best version of yourself. Come join me in the Unstoppable Influence and Our Gathering Table communities, where you will receive all the inspiration you need.

✦ Acting on an opportunity helps you make the leap to additional challenges. You are not WEAK; in fact, you are STRONG!

FREE YOURSELF

1. Make a list of all the times you were told "You can't do that" or you were afraid but you did it anyway and were successful.

2. Every time you unleash your inner strength, add to the list and watch it grow as you grow.

3. Make a list of your accomplishments and put a star by your favorites. Be proud of your accomplishments. You have earned the right to be proud of yourself. Kudos!

CHAPTER 6

FROM CONTROLLING TO TRUSTING

by Christine Hoy

You will keep in perfect peace all who trust in you, all whose thoughts are fixed on you! Trust in the Lord always, for the Lord God is the eternal Rock.

— Isaiah 26:3–4 (NLT)

Not too long ago, our dear friends from South Africa visited us for several weeks. Wanting to be helpful, they started doing the dishes after dinner. You would think I would be grateful, but when they weren't looking, I would sneak back to the kitchen and redo everything.

I was beside myself. I mean, seriously freaked out. It was terrible. Here they were just trying to help, and I was having an emotional meltdown (only visible to my husband...or so I thought). All I knew was that I wanted them out of my kitchen. It was downright embarrassing, but I didn't know how to stop myself, *how to let go.*

Do you sometimes feel like you need to do everything yourself because no one else can do it the way you think it should be done?

Do you always feel the need to be right?

When was the last time you "lost it" because something didn't go your way?

Has anyone ever referred to you as a "control freak"?

I confess: "Hello. My name is Christine, and I struggle with control issues."

This wasn't the first time in our eight-year marriage that dishes were a source of emotional upheaval for me. When we were newlyweds, my husband Brian invited me to watch a movie with him after dinner one evening. I protested because I hadn't done the dishes yet. He assured me it was all right. I could do them later.

Halfway through the movie, he paused it to go make popcorn. While he was waiting for it to pop, he decided to put the dishes in the dishwasher. I heard the noise and went flying up the stairs to the kitchen, certain he must be angry.

(Brian had never given me cause to believe he might be angry about something like this. But based on old patterns from a previous relationship, I made an incorrect assumption about his feelings.)

I begged him, "Please…STOP!"

He couldn't understand why I was so upset. It seemed completely logical to him to do the dishes while waiting for the popcorn. What seemed *illogical* was his wife having a meltdown from what most would consider a helpful gesture.

The next night after dinner, he pulled up a chair near the dishwasher and made me sit and watch him do dishes. It was excruciating! The dishes were supposed to be *my* job. This was again based entirely on experience. If my first husband did the dishes, it was because he was angry that I hadn't done them in a timely manner. This was why I experienced a trauma response when I heard Brian doing what I had previously believed was my sole responsibility.

In that moment, I became aware of the root of my need for control: I feared *criticism*. As a recovering perfectionist and people pleaser, I was afraid of messing up. It was also the root of my tendency to procrastinate. I feared that I might not do it correctly.

Throughout my life, not measuring up earned me loads of criticism. I learned to walk on eggshells, and letting go of old patterns proved to be very difficult. I wanted to make others happy so they would like and approve of me. I wanted to feel loved.

I discovered another underlying reason for my need to control people and situations: insecurity about my own shortcomings. *What if they judge me?*

I'm super self-critical because I tend to have unrealistic expectations for myself. I used control as a means to protect myself from criticism and judgment.

After my latest dishwashing meltdown, I knew I needed to let God transform this area of my life. I was desperate to change and started with an open, transparent conversation with my sweet husband.

He prayed with me, and I knew I needed to have a frank discussion with our guests explaining why I was such a mess. I apologized for the way I had handled the situation. They were gracious, and I felt so relieved I had been open and honest with them.

This led me to set some intentions for myself, which have proven to be very helpful as I began to release my need for control.

I started to...

+ **Ask myself why I feel a need to control a specific situation.** Do I feel threatened? Defensive? Afraid? Awareness is key to change.

+ **Be patient rather than react to every little thing.** For instance, watching my dear husband set the dirty dog dish on the kitchen counter without reprimanding him. *Eww...gross.* But it's not my place to judge. I've had to learn to accept a different level of clean than the one I was brought up with. (To be fair, I was raised by a mother who had severe OCD. I come by my germaphobia honestly.)

✦ **Let others do things in their own way and in their own time.** Like making the bed. I used to drive my husband crazy by demanding he fluff the pillows and place them neatly on the bed. When I was growing up, my mother would double check to make sure I had made nice, crisp hospital corners and all the wrinkles were out. My grandmother even insisted I iron my own sheets when I spent summers with her.

✦ **Stop needing to always be right.** Yeah, that was me. *Every single time.* I found it impossible to drop something when it was clear I was in the right. However, I have learned it is better to be kind.

✦ **Listen more instead of jumping to conclusions or giving advice.** I am not saying I never offer advice anymore, but I try to pause and observe before I ask if it's okay to suggest another way of doing something. Far more often, I am learning to just trust that another person's way of doing something is okay.

✦ **Let go of things I can't control.** When we decided to move from Michigan to North Carolina, we were under contract for a house in the mountains. I had mentally moved in! On our way to North Carolina for inspections, our realtor called to say the deal had fallen through. I felt like I'd been punched in the gut. I prayed, "Lord, I trust you…" repeatedly. It was all I could get out. But a few days later, we discovered that an even better house was available, and we realized God had been trying to protect us from making a bad decision.

✦ **Put more of my trust in God, instead of myself.** I have grown to love Isaiah 26:3-4 [NLT], "You will keep in *perfect peace* all who *trust* in you, all whose *thoughts* are fixed on you! *Trust* in the Lord always, for the Lord God is the *eternal Rock.*" (Emphasis mine.) If I set aside my anxieties and fears, trusting God to fill me with His thoughts, I will experience "perfect peace." No matter what else happens, I can rest in the security of knowing He loves me and there are no criteria I need to meet to be worthy of that love.

When we traveled to Israel several years ago, our guide would start off each day by saying, "Let's see what the Lord has for us today." We would not know from day to day what the itinerary was. And because of the unrest in the country, the guide had to stay fluid in his plans as well.

Even though I still love to have an idea of what the plan is, I use it more as a place to start. When there's a change, I experience a momentary sense of panic, and then I say to myself, "I wonder what God has for me instead?"

My friend (and my former pastor's wife) texted me while I was writing this chapter and asked me to pray for them. They were supposed to be embarking on an Alaskan cruise the next day to celebrate their wedding anniversary. However, they had driven four hours to Detroit only to discover that their flight to Seattle had been canceled. Not delayed. She was scared they would miss their opportunity to enjoy this much-anticipated trip. I offered up a prayer on their behalf and told her to keep me updated.

The next morning, they were still in Detroit but had managed to secure the #2 and #3 positions on the stand-by list. This time, I texted back a prayer asking God to provide a way for them to make their flight in time to catch their cruise. I wrote, "God, if you have something better for them, we pray you will reveal it to them now."

Minutes later, she sent me screenshots of two boarding passes, which had just popped up on her Delta app. Not only were they going to make their flight, but God had also bumped them up to first class! This was yet another reminder to me of God's faithfulness and my need to trust.

While I still fight the urge to be in control, I am learning that the most important thing to control is my reactions. Since my thoughts and beliefs determine how I respond to all the unexpected disruptions that threaten my orderly world, intentionally releasing my worries and fears to God frees me from the feeling of needing to do everything myself. This allows me to stay calm and go with the flow.

I challenge you to practice letting go of control. Trust others to do things their way. Be patient, gentle, and kind. Stop needing to always be right. And instead learn to release your worries to God. If you do this regularly, you too can experience unshakable peace in your life.

KEY TAKEAWAYS

✦ Become aware of where your need for control is rooted.

✦ Talk with someone you trust and feel safe with about your desire to change. Together you can come up with a plan to start trusting.

✦ When things don't go your way, stop and ask yourself, "I wonder what God has for me instead?" or, "What lesson is God trying to teach me through this experience?"

✦ You may not be able to control every situation, but you do have control over your thoughts and how you respond to the unexpected disruptions that threaten your orderly world.

FREE YOURSELF

1. Ask yourself whether you or anyone close to you would say you struggle with control issues. If the answer is *yes*, reflect on a specific time you felt a need to be in control. Journal about this situation until you figure out the underlying fear.

2. What would happen if you released it? Who do you need to start trusting? How would you potentially benefit from choosing not to stress over things out of your control?

CHAPTER 7

FROM LOST TO FOUND

by Christine L. Stallard

Sometimes we must lose ourselves to find ourselves.

— Sonny Long

I thought leaving my career of more than 30 years would be easy. After all, I was stressed out, burned out, and had stayed way past my expiration date.

That's what I told everyone, including myself.

Instead, leaving a high-profile government affairs career that I was very passionate about became the first step on the path to losing myself. From a financial perspective I was prepared, but I hadn't given one thought to how it would affect me mentally and emotionally.

That was a huge mistake.

An identity crisis doesn't happen overnight. And it leaves clues. I missed all of them and never saw the train wreck coming.

Looking back, I can say without a shadow of a doubt that it all started the minute I announced my retirement date. I gave the organization several months' advance notice so we could select my replacement and prepare the organization for a smooth transition.

A piece of my identity left with each responsibility and project I turned over to my replacement. The pièce de résistance was suggesting he move into my office. I thought I'd be just fine in a tiny office space near the back door of the building.

As it turned out, I wasn't. (Imagine that.)

Looking back, I realize that the people and circumstances of my life had defined me up to that moment. I allowed it to happen, and I rather liked the person I had become.

But all that was changing.

If I had paid attention to the emotional alarms that were going off like rapid fire, and if retirement had been the only life-changing event at the time, the transition may have gone more smoothly.

But two months after I retired, my husband and I found ourselves under mandatory evacuation orders for five weeks as a wildfire raged to within two miles of my dream home. That meant I had to be ready to leave immediately, with or without notice.

We watched the fire from a nearby ridge every day, navigated National Guard and state patrol checkpoints almost daily, and watched fire crews appear out of nowhere to check the property for defensibility should we (God forbid) have to evacuate.

We were never forced to leave, but the whole somewhat surreal experience triggered off-the-charts stress.

Five months later, we sold my dream home when it wasn't even on the market. We had put the For Sale sign up just before I retired because my husband felt it was time for us to downsize. Much as I hated to admit he was right, I knew deep in my heart that it was time.

But with everything else happening in my life, my home had become my anchor. When we took it off the market for the winter, I was so relieved. Then, during a freak snowstorm (as we were packing for a trip to the Caribbean), my real estate agent called and said he had a buyer. Just like that, my anchor was gone, and I was completely adrift.

I joke about it now, saying we were "homeless," but we weren't. We had an incredible opportunity to move in with family. With only 45 days to move and no idea how long it would take to find our next home, we quickly had to decide what would go into long-term storage and what we'd take.

A piece of my identity was sealed in each box I packed at home, similar to what had happened when I'd boxed up my office. It was déjà vu. This time, when the moving van pulled out of our driveway, it went "POOF" just like Houdini.

All I had left were boxes of my favorite books that had once sat neatly on my library shelves. Boxes that held my office supplies and files. Boxes with canned and dry food that had once been meticulously organized in the pantry.

We loaded our bed, the dog beds, a few sets of clothes, the library, pantry, and office boxes into the U-Haul and closed that chapter of our lives. Not knowing where I'd find space for my quilting studio, I also loaded my sewing machine and a quilt project I had to finish for a wedding. (The rest of my closetful of quilting fabric went to storage, which is every quilter's worst nightmare.)

We lived surrounded by this fortress of boxes for 10 months.

I've struggled with panic attacks most of my life, but they had increased in frequency and now often appeared out of nowhere. Specifically, I remember unsuccessfully trying to find an extra jar of Dijon mustard I knew was in one of the pantry boxes I had opened for the hundredth time. Instead of putting Dijon on the shopping list, I had a complete meltdown.

Most people know that left unchecked, anxiety and stress will affect your mental and physical health, but what I didn't realize at the time is that it can also affect everyone around you, including your animals.

My husband, friends, and family were concerned and tried to help. But when my behavior caused Kaya (our female Bouvier des Flandres) to suffer a dog's version of a nervous breakdown and nearly die, I knew it was time to pull myself together for everyone's sake.

I decided that the stack of personal development books I had recently accumulated was a good place to start. I began journaling my thoughts, lost myself in music, and surrounded myself with a community of positive, supportive people (including many I met online).

In my rediscovery, I realized I had allowed the people and circumstances of my career to define my life and me. But that was now in the past. All that was left was the dark void of the unknown. I was lost.

I couldn't seem to let go of the past, even though I needed to, because some of it was truly way past its expiration date. I have no problem tossing the outdated things in the refrigerator. But for some reason, when it came to getting rid of the outdated things in my head, I just couldn't do it.

Deep down inside, I knew I had more to offer the world, but my mind was telling me that I was too old. That if I tried something new, I would fail.

So I continued to dig deep into my soul and rediscovered interests and passions I had long since forgotten. I studied how the mind works, learned how powerful it is, and realized the importance of mastering it.

Life had thrown me a bunch of curveballs. My thoughts were running wild, and it was time to harness the power of my mind and stop the downward spiral.

On my journey of discovery, the idea of looking at my life story as a book with chapters and pages came to me. I realized my life wasn't over, it was simply time for me to turn the page, to design and live a new chapter.

So I turned the page, discovering four key actions that helped provide the foundation for designing my next chapter.

First, I started each day with a grateful heart. I found if you focus on the great things that happened in the past and are happening in the present, you can't help but shift your mindset from what's lacking to what's abundantly possible.

Next, I journaled my thoughts, which made all the difference in mastering my mind. I could see where my inner critic was sabotaging me and also what happened when I was able to push her aside and go for it.

I also tried to ground myself in the present (still a work in progress) because the reality is, the past is gone and cannot be changed. And the future isn't here yet, so worrying about it is just a waste of time.

Finally, I asked God for guidance, patience, and peace, which aren't easy for me. I've been labeled a "control freak" on more than one occasion, and patience was never one of my virtues. So relinquishing control of the outcome and waiting for the next steps to be revealed was a challenge.

And peace? Given my propensity for panic attacks, let's just say that wasn't going to happen overnight either.

But once I tapped into all the positive energy surrounding me, learned to let go of the past, and put trust and faith in God's plan, I found my way. Funny how that goes.

I realize now that the transition allowed me to find a new, and in some ways better, version of myself.

I learned that my identity is not my career. It's within myself.

And I learned that to transition and start a new chapter meant I first had to let go of what no longer fit (and wasn't so awesome anyway) with the season of life I had moved into.

When I turned the page, I didn't have a clue what I would write in my next life chapter. But I knew I wanted to weave all my awesome life experiences, strengths, uniqueness, dreams, and desires into a beautiful new chapter that included a more authentic version of myself.

I took a gigantic step outside my comfort zone to pursue new dreams and desires.

I am now a Certified Personal Empowerment Coach. I wrote an Amazon best-selling book called *Your Next Chapter: Dream It. Design It. Live It.* And I regularly write about my experiences, mindset tips, and a roadmap to help others transition from a career they are no longer passionate about to a next, best chapter of life.

My personal experience with the devastating effects that extreme stress can inflict on an entire family, in combination with my passion for sharing the lessons learned from Kaya's near demise, led me to a certification in animal aromatherapy.

My life is unfolding according to God's plan and is better than expected. I am no longer lost. I found an even better version of myself.

Life is a unique, amazing journey—full of ups and downs, good times and bad. Every end along the way is also a beginning.

When you can master your mind, you can better navigate the tough times, face your fear of the unknown, and then turn the page to a new beginning when it's time.

You won't be lost. You'll design a new, amazing chapter and your true, authentic self will step confidently into it.

KEY TAKEAWAYS

✦ Your identity is not defined by your career. It is within you.

✦ If left unchecked, stress and anxiety can affect your mental and physical health as well as the health of those around you.

✦ A life transition requires planning from mental and emotional perspectives, as well as a financial one.

✦ The mind is powerful. It can either open your heart and soul to new opportunities or sabotage your every effort to change and leave you stuck in the past.

✦ Your life story is a book with chapters and pages. Your life isn't over when one chapter ends. You simply need to turn the page, pick up the pen, and design a new, awesome one.

FREE YOURSELF

Every person is on their own transformational journey, and that is their unique story. What's your story? Write it down so you can leave what no longer serves you in the past where it belongs, change your routines, and begin to create new habits so you can move forward.

Here are some questions to get you started.

1. How did people and events influence your professional and personal life?

2. What limiting beliefs, inner critic "chatter," or untruths are sabotaging your plans for the future?

3. What behaviors and habits are sabotaging your plans for the future? Do these truly make life better, or are they just false beliefs?

CHAPTER 8

FROM SCARED TO CONFIDENT

by Colleen Rekers

*The beautiful thing about fear is, when you run
to it, it runs away.*

— **Robin Sharma**

As a little girl with long curls flowing down my back, a checkered school uniform, and Mary Janes, I dreamed of having a big family, a white picket fence, and the most amazing marriage. As an only child and over-achiever, I was raised with high expectations and was loved immensely, yet I never felt good enough. I always strived for the unattainable goal of being "perfect" and having the "perfect life."

In law school, I met a handsome man who loved me for me, imperfections and all. After seven years together, we got married and started our dream life. We had a lot of fun, but our marriage was not without its challenges. Among other things, we struggled to start a family, which was heartbreaking for me because I had always wanted to be a mom.

Eventually, we were blessed with twins…and two years later, with triplets.

I felt like all my dreams were coming true—until addiction tore my marriage apart. Before I knew it, I was a single mom of five children in diapers. I was beyond scared—I was terrified.

I had the most beautifully perfect children, but I was far from perfect. No longer did I have the "perfect" life I had always dreamed of.

I remember retreating to my room at the end of each night after all the children were in bed. I would softly close the bedroom door and fall to my knees in uncontrollable tears. Thoughts swirling in my head…

*I'm exhausted. I've failed. How the f**k am I going to do this?*

I love my children so much, and I don't want them to suffer. They don't have an able father, but how can I be both a father and a mother?

How can I give them everything they need? How can they want for nothing? How am I going to afford to raise them on my own?

Why me? What did I do wrong?

I can't do this—I just can't!

The negative thoughts continued. Sometimes I never even made it to bed. My body would give out before my mind would stop, and I'd fall asleep on the floor in a pile of tears.

Despite my intense fear, which led to the onset of adult anxiety, panic attacks, and depression, I never allowed my children to see my struggle. Those around me characterized me as a strong, confident, got-it-all-together Supermom.

Meanwhile, I struggled in silence, keeping my immense love for my children at the forefront. It was a love so deep and strong that it lifted me up, even in the darkest of moments.

Winston Churchill said, "Fear is a reaction. Courage is a decision."

When my children were toddlers, my fear grew. I had several medical issues, in addition to being 100+ pounds overweight from lack of self-care due to my years in survival mode.

One warm summer day, I was watching my children play in the water outside and my laughter ceased...under my sunglasses, I could feel my eyes water and the tears roll down my cheeks. It came to me like a black cloud: my children only had me.

Their father was in the height of addiction, struggling to take care of just himself. I was an only child with very little family. My father had passed, and my mother was limited in the help she could offer us.

Up to this point, I had never asked for help. I had never created a support system because I didn't want to burden anyone. Instead, I found ways to do everything on my own and continue this illusion of unattainable perfection, pretending that I was "all good" and didn't need anything from anybody.

That day, I made what was ultimately a life-changing decision. It was the first step in what became an avalanche of changes that moved me out of the abyss of fear to an authentic confidence where I could honestly declare, "I got this!"

I realized that life is not meant to be perfect and that *everyone* experiences their own set of obstacles. Without those hard times, no contrast exists to help us experience and appreciate true joy and happiness.

There will always be hard times—there will be cracks, and sometimes large crevasses. However, we can choose to grow through the hard because we can all do hard things. That is what brings us to the light at the end of the tunnel.

After my big epiphany, I continued moving through my fear, step-by-step. I made the effort to build relationships. I sought community. I began to open my mind and heart to others and learn from them and their life experiences.

I researched tools, moved my body, and changed my thinking about how I chose to fuel my body. Despite the extra pounds I carried, I ran a 5K with my twins. Instead of being on the sidelines, I chose to participate, no matter what!

I became a student of life and of the mind. I found what worked and what didn't. I was open to new tools, ways of thinking, and experiences. I worked on healing myself so that I could show up stronger, wiser, and filled with joy for my family.

As my confidence increased, my fear began to subside.

As I did the work, I accumulated a wealth of examples of personal success, which started to outweigh the swirls of negative thoughts in my mind. Good things were happening, and I could feel it on the inside and see it on the outside as I shed over 150 pounds.

Not only did I change my own life, I also changed the lives of my children and ended a cycle of generational negative thinking, anxiety, and depression.

When we heal ourselves, those around us reap the benefits as well.

Rather than sitting in fear, I challenged myself to move outside my comfort zone and into action, and I encourage you to do the same. Life will never be perfect or without challenge, but how you show up—how you react and cope with obstacles that come your way—is your choice, your decision.

As I repeatedly practiced the skills, my confidence began to increase, and I gained momentum. So will you.

Working on yourself is not easy. Many choose not to do it or give up before they reach success. Often they blame the process, the coach, or lack of time, or they claim that they are different, and it just doesn't "work for them."

I'm living proof that bettering yourself CAN work, if YOU do the work.

The most gratifying part of this journey was once again running a 5K with my children years later and carrying a lot less weight on my body and in my mind.

My daughter, with tears in her eyes, said, "Mom, I'm so proud of YOU! Thank you!" As wonderful of a mom as I was back then, I'm an even better mom today because of my journey. And I am truly living my best (perfectly imperfect) life, one filled with joy on the inside and out.

Best of all—while moving from "scared" to "confident," I found my passion and my purpose in leading others through their obstacles and toward their light, with proven tools and techniques that are easy for anyone to implement.

As I look back now, I'm proud of the mom I was then and now. I also realize that I didn't have to suffer alone in silence. I didn't have to bear the challenges and the fear on my own.

And neither do you.

I encourage you to stay open, and don't deprive yourself of success by making excuses for not doing the work. Those who truly decide, who make that choice to go all in and do the work, reap the benefits for themselves and their families.

I challenge you to begin thinking differently about the obstacles that present themselves along your journey. They may look different than mine, and you may not believe things can change. However, I can tell you that we're more alike than you know, and it's never too late to rewrite your story or turn the page to your next chapter.

Do you lack belief in yourself today? It's okay. You can borrow mine until you grow that belief in yourself because I believe in you, and I know that you too can make the shift from scared to confident!

KEY TAKEAWAYS

✦ It's never too late to make a change. It doesn't matter your age or what experiences and obstacles you have faced; you have the ability to make a life-changing decision today.

✦ Fear can propel you forward once you recognize that you have it within you to take that first step.

✦ You don't have to do it alone. As it's been said, it takes a village. We are meant to support and lean on each other to excel, achieve, and live to our fullest.

✦ No matter how immense your struggle feels, you can build the confidence and courage to rise above the fear by taking things one step at a time.

FREE YOURSELF

1. Choose an area of your life to start with, decide to do the work, and commit to taking action. Create an action plan to hold yourself accountable.

2. Implement: Once you have decided, step out of your comfort zone and go all in! Fully immerse and stay true to the decision and commitment you made to yourself.

3. Rinse & Repeat: Evaluate your successes and failures to see what worked and what didn't. Rinse out that which didn't serve you, add more of what you need, then repeat! Seek guidance if needed to help you navigate the process and to maximize your results.

CHAPTER 9

FROM SCARED TO BRAVE

by Donna Connor

Our deepest fear is not that we are inadequate. Our deepest fear is that we are powerful beyond measure. It is our light, not our darkness that most frightens us.

— **Marianne Williamson**

When I was in the sixth grade, my teacher always said he thought I would grow up to be a girl Friday: a female assistant entrusted with a wide variety of tasks. I was always the girl who volunteered to help or run errands for him. I loved getting out of the classroom!

My first job, at the age of 16, was riding an ice cream bike for Sea World in San Diego. I loved it! When I graduated high school, I had absolutely no idea what I wanted to do. I signed up for junior college, taking basic classes, and worked as a cashier at the liquor store on a naval base. Then at the age of 19, I ran off to Texas with a guy.

My resume at that time included riding a bike and selling liquor. I didn't have much hope getting a "real" job with those skills. But as the saying goes, "It's not what you know, it's *who* you know."

I was living with a family in Texas taking care of their kids in exchange for room and board. They were kind and helped me find a job to pay my bills. They reached out to a friend who owned a construction business and was looking for a receptionist. He was very nice and hired me even though I didn't have any experience. I only worked for him for six months, but I was grateful for all I learned in this position.

I then moved to Utah and did various jobs from cashiering to being an undercover security operative at a department store to being a receptionist at a mortuary. I just floated around from job to job. Each job was unique though and provided me with the variety I needed. I learned something from every position that I could use in the next, and I was able to elevate my position with each job I took.

I eventually found a great position as an office administrator, where I stayed for 10 years. I learned skills such as accounting and human resources administration. I got an education thanks to their tuition reimbursement program and made a lot of connections that would later serve me well.

During this time, I had a strong feeling that I was supposed to do more with my life. I felt a strong entrepreneurial itch that I didn't know how to scratch. I threw a lot of ideas at the wall and tried to see what would stick, but nothing really panned out. I LOVED the creativity of starting a business—writing a business plan, designing a logo, dreaming about it, creating processes—but I got scared when it came time to launch.

For 15 years, I was a dreamer, not a finisher. I would work SO hard for months getting ready to launch a product or a training, but I could NEVER push the launch button. I would never put it out there to the world.

I was great at making money for other people and running their businesses, but I couldn't seem to do it for myself. I was just too scared.

Over the years, I spent a lot of time and money on ventures that I was passionate about in the beginning, but I didn't have the interest to do what it took every day to make them successful.

Out of all my entrepreneurial attempts, only one truly worked for me. I had taken accounting classes at my previous job, so when their accountant retired, I was able to quit my job and take over as their new one.

Over the next 12 years, I worked from home and loved that I could control my hours. My client base grew, and my accounting business was successful and satisfying. However, I started hating the fact that if I didn't work, I wouldn't get paid. Sure, I could have built a team of other accountants or bookkeepers, but the thought of having other people relying on me to cover their bills scared me to death.

So I stayed a solopreneur for 10 long years.

Throughout this time, I still felt strongly that I should be doing something more. I just had absolutely no idea what that "more" was! Then one day it hit me. I knew *exactly* what I wanted to do!

I discovered what I was passionate about, what felt like a true calling. This time I wasn't just throwing another idea out there wondering if it would work. I knew this would drive me past the creation stage. This was it... and it scared me to death!

I was scared of failing again. I was scared to put myself out there. I was scared of being judged. I was scared of losing more money. Because let's face it, based on my track record, I had a lot of "proof" in my own mind that I wasn't a successful person. I had tried so many things in the past that hadn't worked—so why should this time be any different?

Instead of taking a leap of faith, my fear took over and I sat on my idea.

I didn't do a single thing.

I had finally found my calling, but I was too scared to act on it. So I shelved the idea because this time it meant something to me. If I started it, I wouldn't allow myself to fail.

I ended up becoming the general manager for one of my accounting clients and shut down my own accounting business. I loved what I was doing and creating as the new general manager. The processes I put in place allowed us to scale our consulting firm.

From time to time, I would get the nudge to go after my calling, but I always allowed fear to stop me from doing anything with it.

Then one day I was scrolling through Facebook, and an ad came up—it was about being an Unstoppable Influencer and making a difference in people's lives. Everything in the ad hit a pain point that spoke to me and said, "This is for me!" So I clicked on the button to learn more.

As it turned out, Natasha Hazlett was hosting a 21-day challenge for people who wanted to become Unstoppable Influencers. I jumped in with both feet.

During the challenge, Natasha spoke about the lies we tell ourselves that are keeping us from making a difference in the world. She had us write down the lies we were telling ourselves and then the proof that they were, in fact, lies.

My three lies were...

A. Who am I to do this thing?

B. I've failed at everything else; I'll ruin this too.

C. Everyone will judge me for doing this and will unfriend me if I post about it to grow my business.

Then I wrote down the evidence that they were lies.

A. I'm the general manager for a multimillion-dollar consulting firm, and I'm successfully scaling it to the next level. I've had a successful accounting practice for 10 years, where I made more money working part-time than I ever did full-time. I know how to create processes to run a successful business. I've been helping people get out of debt for 13 years. I took my mess and did something with it to help others. I've been led to make connections with many people that I would need to make this come to pass. I have learned every skill I need to make this a success from other things I've done in my life.

B. The truth is, I haven't failed at anything. I quit working on things that didn't fulfill me. The one that did fulfill me was very successful. The reason I didn't launch those things is because I wasn't passionate about doing them long-term.

C. People are going to judge me no matter what. Why not let them judge me for going after my dreams instead of hiding? Why not really go for it? Who cares what they think anyway? Their judgment is more about them than it is about me.

Can I tell you a secret?

I cried like a baby after this exercise. I couldn't believe these three silly lies had kept me from going after what I knew I was supposed to do.

And so...I went for it! I got my brave on. I found the right coaches who could get me where I wanted to go, and now I'm going after my dreams. I LOVE what I'm doing! I'm making a difference in people's lives. I've gone from Scared to Brave. I've become a financial advisor, a certified coach in several modalities, and a best-selling author! Best of all, I have no problem growing my business through social media now.

Has it been easy? No. Has it been perfect? No. Have I stumbled a lot? You betcha!

But after every setback, I learn from it and keep moving forward. I no longer allow mistakes to push me back into scared mode. I can see them for what they are—opportunities for growth—and I keep "braving on."

Best of all, I'm showing my family how to truly go after their dreams no matter what gets in their way. I am PROUD of who I am and who I am becoming. I went from being scared to becoming brave to finally seeing the success I always dreamed about! If I can do it, you can do it too.

KEY TAKEAWAYS

✦ If you find yourself struggling, it may be due to lies in your mind that are stopping you from succeeding.

✦ People are going to judge you no matter what. Why not let them judge you for going after your dreams instead of hiding?

✦ Get your brave on and go for it!

FREE YOURSELF

1. Is there something you feel you should be doing in life but certain thoughts are keeping you from doing them and living an unstoppable life? What are they?

2. What are the lies you are telling yourself? What are the truths to those lies?

3. Once you can clearly see they are lies, you will be liberated from the fear that has been holding you back and will have the power to be brave enough to go for it!

CHAPTER 10

FROM NOT ENOUGH TO A GIFT

by Ellie West

And I will keep reminding myself, every moment, that I matter. That I am worthy. That I am enough. I will keep reminding myself until the truth seeps into my flesh and finds its home nestled amongst my bones. Until the truth always knows the way home.

— Becca Lee

I remember the moment clearly. I was in the second grade, sitting at my desk alone next to the wall and blackboard. Everything else around me was entirely black. Little did I know that I was experiencing the first of several false labels being embedded in my spirit.

How did I get to that lonely place?

My class had two reading groups: the good readers and those who struggled. I vividly remember being pulled

aside by my second-grade teacher and put into the re-
medial reading group with only a few students.

As the teacher led us out of the classroom, I looked back
at my classmates sitting in their reading circle, and a
feeling of sadness overcame me. A sadness I didn't fully understand at the time. I felt…different.

What my teachers and parents didn't know at the time
was that I was being sexually abused. My dark secret created shame and guilt and was the root of my
struggles at school. I felt alone and embarrassed that
I couldn't fully participate in school. I had a myriad
of feelings and emotions swirling inside me from the
abuse, which I couldn't possibly understand at that tender age.

Instead, I began believing that I wasn't smart enough.

As I made my way through school, I had another experience a few years later that created yet another false
label. I cannot remember what I said or did at the time,
but my music teacher asked me to stand up and come
forward. I was shaking as I walked to the front of the
class. He handed me a dunce hat and told me to put it
on and stand in the corner facing my peers. It was one
of my most horrifying experiences.

I remember feeling embarrassed, ashamed, not smart
enough, and not good enough. As I walked home, tears

streamed down my face. On that day, another false belief became deeply rooted inside me: I wasn't good enough. I didn't dare share this experience with anyone for fear of what they might say.

These labels of not being smart enough or good enough grew with me as I got older, leading me to compare myself with others constantly.

I was athletically blessed and found tremendous joy in playing tennis and running long-distance. Since it seemed that I wasn't smart enough or good enough to succeed in school, I figured I would focus on being a great athlete. With each game I played and each race I ran, I became more determined to be the best.

I soon learned that my personal best did not necessarily make me THE best.

Karen was the star of our tennis team. She won numerous tournaments and was eventually inducted into our High School Tennis Hall of Fame. No matter how much I played or practiced, I could never beat Karen.

Laurie was an exceptional runner. I was always behind her. I could never catch up—she always crossed the finish line before me.

Throughout the years, I compared myself to Karen and Laurie. I fell into the comparison and competition trap. Before long, my false labels had compounded into...

I'm not smart enough.

I'm not good enough.

I'm not fast enough.

In hindsight, I realize that I was trying to find my value and worth based on my relationships with others. It was a game I would never win. One that would always leave me feeling like I was coming up short—never "enough."

One day, my mom told me, "Ellie, you are so unique."

I never forgot that comment. For many years, I was hurt by it because I felt it was a judgment. I thought she was comparing me to one of my aunts. My aunt was vocal, bold, and negative, and I didn't want to be like her.

Unfortunately, my mom died before I could ask what she had meant by that statement. Yet the beauty of her words years later led me on a journey of self-discovery, homing in on my uniqueness, gifts, and purpose.

I have since learned that there are several areas where we are gifted to be uniquely and beautifully ourselves. We have our personalities, core values, strengths (and weaknesses), spiritual gifts, and unique stories. Our Creator masterfully thought out everything about us even before we were born.

Unique Personality

We are all born with unique personalities. As a part of my self-discovery journey, I took numerous personality assessments. I discovered that being an introvert brought its own set of insecurities.

I often thought I *should be* more extroverted. Some may think I am an extrovert because of my distinguished career as a flight attendant, but I can assure you I'm an introvert. I love my alone time and being with a few close friends; it is how I recharge.

Unique Strengths

We have each been equipped with particular strengths and skill sets.

Over time, I have made a point to understand my unique strengths. The CliftonStrengths assessment (formerly StrengthsFinder) was one such tool that allowed me to uncover and appreciate my top five strengths.

To be honest, when I heard of other people's results, I often thought, *I wish that was my strength*. But I've since learned to embrace the well-thought-out strengths and gifts I have been given.

My #1 strength is empathy, followed by connectedness. Once I learned of my top two strengths, I was relieved and began to see and understand my gifts and who I am at the core.

My strengths and gifts were specifically given to me for a greater purpose. For example, I love serving others, whether in the air or on the ground, and I now realize that serving others IS one of my gifts. Embracing my unique strengths and gifts has allowed me to open my heart to serve others more tangibly.

Your Differences Are Your Unique Gifts

I discovered that I needed to stop comparing myself to others or wishing I had their talents. I simply could not compare my gifts with anyone else's.

Just because you're unique doesn't mean you aren't needed or valued—it means quite the opposite. Your difference IS the value you bring to the world.

Each of us was created with a purpose we can use to make the most significant impact. Many times we take for granted things that come very naturally, instead of recognizing them as our gifts and talents.

For example, I would hear and read comments such as…

"You have such a gift in hospitality."

"You are engaging with our passengers."

"You are so good at what you do!"

I would view those comments as "It's just who I am," never really thinking that what I was offering naturally to others in the form of hospitality was my gift or talent.

The gifts and talents we receive from God include skills, abilities, teaching, experiences, encouragement, compassion, faith, and more. You may be familiar with the Parable of the Talents in Matthew 25:14-30. The lesson from that parable is that we should use whatever we have been given for God's purposes. Uncover the gifts and talents you have been given, and do your best to use and expand them.

We're all given a talent. It doesn't matter what gifts or talents you start with; your responsibility is to multiply what you've been given. If you don't use your talent, and instead bury it, what you have will be taken from you and given to those who are more productive. God does not equip people with identical or equal gifts; you should use the talents and gifts you have been given.

I now know that I am enough. I can now see my gifts, and I seek to use them regularly to make an impact in the world.

It is my hope that through the story of my transformation from feeling "not enough" to seeing myself as a "gift" that you see that you too are the perfect, unique part of a larger body of functionality and purpose. Your differences are what make you beautiful. YOU are loved and valued just the way you are. You are a gift!

KEY TAKEAWAYS

✦ You have been created on purpose *for* a purpose.

✦ You are unique, gifted, beautiful, worthy, and valued.

✦ You are enough!

FREE YOURSELF

Finish this sentence: I am a gift because…

CHAPTER 11

FROM DEFICIENT TO PROFICIENT

by Karen Kahn

*You can be pitiful, or you can be powerful, but
you can't be both.*

— Joyce Meyer

My feelings of deficiency stemmed from an experience in kindergarten that I *wasn't even present for* but that my mother had told me about many times.

My mother had sat across from my teacher, Mrs. Fawcett, who was holding a printout of test scores. One little boy was expected to test at the genius level. It showed, just as expected, this boy's very high score.

"But we weren't expecting this..." She pointed to one score, lower than the boy's but much higher than the others...mine.

She looked at my mother. "Mrs. Kahn, I have one question: Why is Karen failing kindergarten?"

The answer was simple but wouldn't reveal itself for another 60 years.

Today there is a lot of information available on autism spectrum disorder (ASD), but teachers back in the 1950s and 1960s weren't taught to recognize the signs. The red flags were present, but my teachers focused on my need for improvement.

In first grade, my teacher wrote: "Karen is still in need of constant attention while daily work is being done. An improvement is necessary."

In second grade, they wrote: "Karen's manuscript writing has not been as neat as possible. Would you stress that her letters be made with care and her papers be neat? Also, Karen is not reading on a second-grade level."

In third grade, they wrote: "Karen is not achieving up to her ability, especially in reading. Writing continues to be messy."

A final comment on my last report card was: "Karen is an interesting child, somewhat difficult to understand."

This same teacher had alerted my parents that my sister Natalie needed her eyes examined. Teachers knew to look for things like that, yet they weren't trained to look for learning disabilities.

This pattern was painfully repeated school year after school year. I was branded with the labels of lazy, unmotivated, and shy. I was told that if I would just apply myself, I could do better.

I dreaded every Report Card Day, knowing what awaited me. My mother would repeat, "I know you are very bright. If you would listen in class, if you would apply yourself and do the work, these grades would improve."

The cycle continued. No matter how hard I tried, my grades never improved.

Having no other explanation, when I asked myself, *What's wrong with me?* the answer that came to mind was, *I guess I'm just stupid.*

School wasn't the only place I found difficult. I struggled in nearly every area of my life.

One vivid memory is when my family went to spend time with close friends at a cabin in the San Jacinto Mountains. One night, I washed my hands at the kitchen sink and tore a paper towel off the roll. In my haste, I accidently tore off two pieces.

My mother said, "You only need one paper towel, Karen. Put one back."

As a seven-year-old on the autism spectrum, I took everything literally. So I froze. My mind went blank. I had no idea how to reattach this extra paper towel back onto the roll.

My mother became impatient and repeated the request. "Put one back!"

All I could do was stand there holding the two paper towels, desperately wanting a solution.

My mother became angry and said, "Karen, you're not stupid. Quit acting this way!"

And I began to cry.

I wasn't acting; I truly didn't understand what was expected of me in that moment.

My learned assumption was that I was, in fact, stupid. This reinforced my belief that I was deficient. As I struggled to function in a world I didn't understand, I felt that I couldn't trust myself or my own perception or judgment because I was always wrong.

In eighth grade, I began to compensate for my dyslexia, and my spelling and reading improved. I graduated with an above-average GPA and went on to do well in college.

Then a much greater challenge loomed before me: breaking free from the self-imposed label "I am deficient."

The issues I faced as an adult were different. I was socially awkward and often found myself standing alone in a crowded room not knowing how to join in on or follow conversations. Often, I'd sit away from the crowd and count the minutes until I could find solitude.

I've heard people say that those on the autism spectrum prefer to be alone, but this is untrue. Most of us want to be included, but we don't know how.

Often, I'd go out with friends knowing I'd be uncomfortable but still wanting to be included. One especially painful evening, I was unable to connect with anyone. Not knowing at the time that I was autistic and that difficulty with social interaction was a characteristic, I thought they just didn't like me.

I would usually come home in tears and ask myself, *What's wrong with me? Why can't I just be normal?*

The answer would fly back in my face: *Because you are less than…not good enough, broken, deficient.*

At the age of 63, I began to research Asperger's Syndrome at my son's suggestion. I was astonished to discover there were others like me, struggling with many of the same issues. This changed everything!

I was not alone in this!

It was as though someone had turned on a bright light in a dark room.

In that moment, the answers to so many lifelong questions flooded my mind…

Why is it so hard for me to connect with people?

Why is it so difficult to function in an atmosphere of noise and confusion?

Why don't I enjoy social events as others do?

The questions were the same, but now the answers were different. There is nothing wrong with me! I'm not broken or deficient. I'm autistic, and these characteristics are normal.

It wasn't long until I had compiled a list of common traits of Asperger's Syndrome that I had struggled with.

◆ Social awkwardness

◆ Difficulty developing and maintaining friendships

◆ Strict adherence to routine, inability to function if the routine is interrupted

◆ Sensory sensitivity

◆ Repetitive motor mannerisms

◆ Difficulty reading social cues

This realization, and eventual diagnoses of ASD, dyslexia, and ADHD, were just the beginning of changes that would come. Rather than use this new information as an excuse, I used it as a springboard to propel myself forward.

Joyce Meyer, a well-respected Christian author and speaker, often tells her audience, "You can be pitiful, or you can be powerful, but you can't be both." I decided that I was going to be powerful.

I became determined to embrace my uniqueness, telling myself, *I'm not defective—I'm unique. I have gifts, talents, and abilities.* After years of doubting myself, I was ready to face this challenge.

I began immersing myself in personal growth and development. In 2018, I was introduced to Natasha Hazlett's book, *Unstoppable Influence: Be You. Be Fearless. Transform Lives.* Since then, I have diligently applied the principles to my life. Namely, I began to decide how I wanted to show up in the world.

This was challenging to implement after spending a lifetime believing I was deficient and repeatedly showing up that way.

My new challenge was to show up as "Proficient Karen." Changing a lifelong pattern wasn't easy, but armed with the new information, I found the courage to move forward with my new label:

I AM PROFICIENT.

My next step was to recognize and maximize my strengths. As I considered situations in the past in which I excelled, I realized I was most comfortable working with people one-on-one, and my years in the ministry had helped me develop qualities of a great life coach.

I had a deep desire to help others excel in life. My mission became twofold: to do the deep work on myself— to identify and release emotional and energetic blocks that were keeping me from becoming all I was meant to be and to help others do the same.

Life as a woman with Asperger's Syndrome did not magically get any easier. I faced difficulties daily. Yet I promised myself that I'd keep moving forward no matter how difficult the situation I faced.

One especially effective tool I discovered to navigate a negative situation quickly was to declare out loud, "I love it!" I put this to the test in 2019, when I flew to attend the Unstoppable Influence Summit. On the way, I became overwhelmed by the noise, crowds, and confusion. Walking through the airport, tears running down my face, I began to say out loud, "I love it!" Uttering this phrase over and over brought me back to an emotionally calm state.

I've learned to recognize and celebrate my wins daily. I record the wins from each day in a journal and acknowledge and applaud myself for even the small wins. This allows me to fall asleep in a positive frame of mind and gives me a tool to use should I become discouraged. Flipping through my journal and remembering past wins raises me to a higher vibration of gratitude and joy.

My path hasn't been easy, but today, that little girl who barely finished kindergarten, who felt deficient, proudly wears her new label of PROFICIENT.

KEY TAKEAWAYS

✦ Embrace your uniqueness. You have gifts, talents, and abilities that lead to a message only you can share with the world.

✦ Keep moving forward. It doesn't matter if you are taking small steps or big leaps, as long as you keep going forward. That is progress and growth!

✦ People do the best they can with the tools and information they are given.

✦ It only takes one piece of information or one profound moment to completely change your life.

FREE YOURSELF

1. Decide how you want to show up in the world. Write it down and hang it somewhere that you'll see every morning.

2. Recognize and celebrate daily wins. This practice takes just a few minutes but yields tremendous results. Each evening, record the wins (both big and small) from that day in a journal, and applaud yourself!

3. Think of one trait or area of your life that you find challenging or anxious about, or that you dislike, and turn it around by saying out loud, "I love it!"

CHAPTER 12

FROM TOTAL TRAIN WRECK TO DIVINELY ALIGNED

by Lisa Cain

You will be a crown of splendor in the Lord's hand, a royal diadem in the hand of your God.

— Isaiah 62:3

In 2015, my world as I knew it collapsed. I felt broken, unloved, and scared for the future I was facing. I would soon be a divorced single parent of two adopted tweens with special needs, while working in a high-stress job. I felt morally, financially, and spiritually bankrupt without much of a clue how to claw my way back to the surface. I acted strong and smiled in public. But when I was alone with my thoughts and feelings, I cried, screamed, and panicked in the dark. I was a total train wreck!

I found myself in a house that was too big for myself and my two kids and debt that felt insurmountable on a single income. I was working a full-time job that required a significant amount of out-of-town travel and had to turn to family for help with supervision of my children. I felt judged for not "making" my marriage work. I was overweight and sleep-deprived, and I drank way too much.

I decided I didn't want to live that way anymore but had no clue where to start. With desperation and anxiety clouding every moment of my day, I was worried about everything.

I knew I needed divine intervention, but I didn't know how to have a relationship with the Lord.

Religion was discouraged in my first marriage, and although I was trying to learn to turn to the Lord for His strength, I had so much confusion about what "faith" meant. I had a strong Catholic background, yet I didn't even know how to pray. I wasn't sure how to seek the Lord with anything other than a memorized prayer, and none of the ones I knew touched on the desperation and fear I felt as 2015 ended and 2016 began.

I decided to start wearing a tiara every Tuesday. At the time, the idea of Tiara Tuesdays seemed to have come out of nowhere. But I now know it was divinely placed on my heart in those quiet moments when I asked for God's guidance. Tiara Tuesdays were the means for the Lord to bring me closer to Him and His plan for me.

When I started wearing tiaras on Tuesdays, they were the only days I felt any sparkle. All the other days, I felt fat, ugly, unloved, unworthy, dumb, incompetent, and so many other labels that I now know were untrue.

On Tuesdays, I curled my hair, put on makeup, and perfectly placed a tiara on my head before facing the day with hope, humor, and borrowed confidence. I smiled and talked with complete strangers about my tiara. It brought eye rolls but also lots of smiles, conversation, and HOPE—for myself and often for those I interacted with.

On Tuesdays, I was open to joy and gratitude. Those positive feelings started to brighten some of my darkest days. I began feeling a renewed connection to my friends, family, and the Lord. I laughed more. And I always knew the next Tuesday was just a few days away.

Tiara Tuesdays spread to friends and colleagues who loved the idea of sparkling for no specific reason. During the next few months, I found my soulmate and embarked on a journey of healing and growth that I hadn't imagined would be possible.

In 2017, my employer encouraged me to stop wearing my tiara, and I respected that request. Tiara Tuesdays were "retired." By that time, I had found the inner strength I had been searching for. I was experiencing a love I had always dreamed about. I learned how to talk with the Lord and pour out my fears, anxieties, and worries so that He could light the path for me to walk.

I triple-dog-dared my fiancé to marry me in early 2017, and instead of continuing to plan our wedding, we eloped the same day. That too was divine intervention because the Lord knew I would need a solid foundation for our new family unit. We decided to find a congregation new to both of us and immediately began visiting local churches each Sunday.

Exactly 43 days after our elopement, our youngest child experienced the first of many mental health crises and was hospitalized. As we visited a congregation shortly after the hospitalization, the Lord spoke hope to my husband and me during a sermon at the church we soon joined. That day, the pastor spoke about children's mental health and the need for personal connection and community. He shared how both could be developed within the church family. God often delivered the perfect message for my husband and me through that pastor over the many months of our child's hospitalizations.

The next two years were filled with pain, fear, worry, and uncertainty. It was more than we thought we could take on many days. Yet the Lord constantly spoke to me through church sermons, Bible passages, and people in my life.

During this difficult time, we prayed, moved our feet, and flourished. The Lord taught me to seek Him and thank Him for both my pain and accomplishments. He also taught me to trust the purpose for my life *and* look for the lessons in each moment. Sometimes the hope came from a new program we were offered, from a new provider with unique insight, or from a new skill that helped us manage situations differently.

When I found Unstoppable Influence in 2019, I heard the one statement that would significantly change my life: Life is not happening TO you; it is happening FOR you. This simple statement set me on the path of self-awareness and growth that God had been preparing for me.

Divorce did not happen to me; it happened *for* me.

Our child's mental health crisis didn't happen to our family; it happened *for* our family.

The death of a loved one didn't happen to me; it happened *for* me.

The job layoff did not happen to me; it happened *for* me.

The lost friendship didn't happen to me; it happened *for* me.

Each of these difficult experiences helped me grow, leave my comfort zone, and see the Lord's constant presence in my life.

This mindset shift allowed me to feel frustration and sadness in my moments of struggle and simultaneously provided the space to be curious about the lesson I would ultimately learn. In those moments, I allowed myself the grace to navigate the most painful of situations and circumstances. I learned to ask for help from the Lord, my husband, family, friends, and professionals.

In the past, I had been too stubborn to reach out for help. I would have struggled in silence or pitied my struggle. It allowed me to find strength in my vulnerability. It also created the belief that everything had a purpose and would bring glory to God. Faith alone carried me through situations that would have otherwise been insurmountable.

In the seven years since Tiara Tuesday's start, I have been blessed to have experienced a multitude of difficult storms that have helped me grow in more ways than I thought possible. Finding my inner sparkle was the first step in finding my faith and my worth.

Through family estrangement, mental health struggles, work crises, job changes, toxic relationships, death, layoffs, a snow-pocalypse, a pandemic, and significant weight gain and loss, the Lord breathed new life in me. I now get to share the lessons I learned with others who are navigating their own personal storms.

The train wrecks in my life opened up a series of opportunities, which the Lord knew would help me grow. He used them to speak to me, to bring me into alignment with my God-given talents, and to show me a new path where He works in partnership with me.

I now actively seek ways to share strategies with parents whose children are experiencing mental health crises, and Tiara Tuesdays have become a way for me to share my sparkle with others.

The power and impact of Tiara Tuesdays is just beginning. Currently, I share daily positive messages and often mail tiaras to friends and their kiddos. I gift them to others during conferences, seminars, and retreats and make sure to have them on hand to share with strangers on Tuesdays so they can sparkle too. This brings me so much joy! And there is so much more to come.

I've learned to experience the storm, anchor my worth in HIS presence, straighten my crown (ahem, tiara), and walk in divine alignment with the Lord.

If you ever feel like your life has become a total train wreck and is spinning out of control, just remember who you are, that life is happening FOR you and not TO you, that you were fearfully and wonderfully made—on purpose and for a purpose. Then straighten your tiara and allow yourself to come into divine alignment with the One who made you.

KEY TAKEAWAYS

✦ Know that your struggle has a purpose. It may just take a while to be revealed.

✦ Turn to the Lord in your moments of desperation; talk to Him and give Him your worries and your fears.

✦ You don't need to suffer alone. Self-sufficiency does not mean isolation. Instead, find your tribe of people to help you navigate these storms.

FREE YOURSELF

1. Write this down: "Life is not happening TO me; it is happening FOR me."

2. Replace the word *it* with anything you are struggling with (your train wreck).

3. Reframe these as positives to show your growth or the potential lesson. For example:

   a. Train Wreck: "All we do is fight at home."

   b. Reframe: "The conflict at home has encouraged me to become a better communicator."

CHAPTER 13

FROM BOSSY TO DECISIVE

by Maria DeLorenzis Reyes

The word bossy can make you feel like you have to stand down. Don't let people misinterpret your strength.

— Alicia Keys

It was a beautiful summer day and I, along with my group of friends, had planned to spend the day swimming at Julie's house. As young teenagers, we often spent the summer days hanging out and doing what girls our age did best. We didn't have any responsibilities yet, no steady jobs or siblings to watch. We were starting high school in the fall, and except for occasional babysitting or chores at home, the days were ours to spend the way we wanted.

I was determined to get over to my friend Julie's house to get into the pool as quickly as possible! Although I didn't have any authority over my friends, I was typically the one everyone looked to for a plan. They would come to me for help and would follow my advice. I'm not sure how it happened, but at some point I became the "chosen one" in my group of friends—likely because no one else would make decisions or take action, but I would.

My friends were taking their time talking and getting ready as the minutes quickly ticked away. It was nearly 2 pm and we hadn't even left to walk over to Julie's house. If we didn't get moving, we weren't going to have much time because we all had to be home for dinner.

After waiting patiently, I finally said, "Let's go, girls—get a move on!"

Most of the group started moving faster and gathering their things. But my friend Kathy said, "Don't be so bossy. You're always bossing us around!" The other girls stayed quiet.

I said, "I'm sorry…I didn't realize I was the problem!"

My other friends told her to stop. She said she was sorry, but her reaction made a strong impact on me.

Throughout my life, people have labeled me "bossy." It had a negative connotation, and I always felt mislabeled.

As a child, I was called "bossy" when I took the lead or made decisions about what we should do or how to do it. I felt that speaking up was how I had to assert myself and get what I needed. As a teen, I started to hide my decisive, assertive manner so I would be liked and not seen as aggressive.

As I grew up, I learned that hiding those traits didn't serve me, and I began a journey back to my natural state. I say it was a "journey" because it took time for me to get back to who I was, taking little steps to begin to assert myself again. I needed to step into it slowly... but once I did, there was no going back!

I recall the moment I claimed the power of that label. Right after college graduation, my friends and I started a tradition of renting a beach house for the summer. We all had just started our careers working in New York City, and the beach was our escape.

On this particular weekend, my roommate Eve and I had returned to the house a little earlier than the rest of the crew. We went to sleep, and the rest of our roommates tumbled in after 3 am with guests who were going to sleep over. They were extremely intoxicated.

Not only were they loud and woke me up, they then proceeded to use the phone in my bedroom. (This was back in the day when there were no cell phones.) They called another group of friends staying in a nearby house. Of course since they were drunk, they were silly, giddy, and acting stupid. While they were having tons of fun, my other roommate and I were not amused; we had just been awakened out of a dead sleep.

The phone calls, loud conversations, and laughs continued. After a while, the party crew turned off the lights and went to sleep, but the other group of friends kept calling our house. Since they were drunk, my friends passed out and stopped answering, so the phone rang incessantly. I was furious.

At the time, I was still struggling to break out of that pattern I had fallen into of not being decisive or taking action to avoid being called "bossy" or "aggressive" and not speaking up for what I needed. Because of that, close to 20 minutes passed as I had an internal fight with myself while that annoying phone just kept ringing. Finally, I just couldn't hold back any longer.

I got up and said, "You guys are obnoxious, and those people need to stop calling here!"

They knew I was pissed off. After a few seconds of them trying to be serious and holding their laughter, I answered the phone and screamed, "You guys need to stop calling already. We're trying to sleep over here!"

I hung up the phone and unplugged it so it wouldn't ring anymore...or at least I thought I had. In my frustration, I had only unplugged the wire that went from the receiver to the device on the wall, so it continued to ring but I couldn't pick it up because it wasn't connected to the handle.

I fumbled with the wire trying to get it reconnected. The whole time I kept screaming, "I can't WAIT to connect this so I can answer! I'm gonna plug this phone back in, and I'm going to tell them off and to STOP CALLING!"

Well, I did exactly that and the ringing finally stopped. It was kind of comical when I think about it, but not at that moment.

The next morning, Eve (who had also been sleeping and awakened by the disruption) said, "Ya know, I saw something different in you last night."

"Really? How so?"

"You used to keep your mouth shut and not speak up for yourself, just take things as they were. But now you're different."

I didn't know Eve prior to college, so she had never seen me in my authentic state, as the person others had called "bossy." She only knew me as a person who didn't speak up for herself in order to be liked. She didn't know me as the person who had begun the journey back to being my authentic self.

That night was a milestone in that journey back to ME, where I claimed the strength of my natural state and refused the label that had been assigned to me.

Bossy has such a negative connotation. That moment was when I said, "No, I'm not bossy. I'm decisive!" Bossy was the negative label I had been given because people didn't like my assertive style. In reality, I was taking action, making decisions, solving problems, speaking up, asking for what I needed, and standing up for others!

That was the pivotal moment when I started to step into the truth of who I am: I am decisive, and that is a strength.

Owning the reframed label of "decisive" was an important part of my journey. In a way, all of those experiences brought me to the place where I owned it all, and that fueled my accomplishments. I stepped into leadership positions throughout my life, leading my peers in projects and initiatives. I was an entrepreneur early, owning my first business in college, and my decisiveness helped me to achieve all that I did. After graduating college, I was able to embrace that strength that others had labeled negatively. I began to use it as a tool and claimed it as my superpower.

Working in the real world as a woman trying to get ahead, I continued with my assertive, aggressive-at-times style. In reality, it served me to succeed in life, in my career, with project work, and leading others in my personal and professional life. I attained success in my career, working up to a leadership position early, which later earned me positions on senior management teams at billion-dollar companies. I was seen as an innovator and problem-solver. I directed and led projects to completion that others had struggled to execute. I was able to make the business case for improvements that helped shape the companies I worked for, leading them to higher levels of success.

When I left the corporate grind, I returned to entrepreneurship again and used those same decisive qualities to build my own business, achieving success to heights I had not imagined before college.

The tenacity from my natural state was reignited, released, and recharged that night at the beach house. It fueled what I accomplished and made me the decisive boss I was meant to be.

It can be tough to fight that inner battle with a label that people tag you with externally. But when you step into that and are able to stand in that strength, not caring how others perceive it, you can celebrate what that looks like and feel proud and confident in the ability to be DECISIVE.

Maybe you've been given the bossy label too. If so, I just want you to know—you are not bossy, you are decisive! That, my friend, is a superpower—so own it!

#banbossy

KEY TAKEAWAYS

✦ Labels can impact the essence of who you are and cause you to change your behavior, to your detriment.

✦ Losing yourself and finding yourself is a process and will lead up to you embracing who you truly are.

✦ Other people may label things they are scared of, or threatened by, because it is uncomfortable for THEM. Accepting or rejecting that is your choice!

✦ What could be perceived as bossy very well may be the strength of being decisive. Bossy is not a flaw, it's a superpower!

FREE YOURSELF

1. Write about times you've been mislabeled. What were some positive things that resulted from that for you, others, or both?

2. Is there an area of your life where you have an opportunity to be decisive, but you've stopped yourself for fear of being mislabeled? Take the first step to being decisive in that area in the next week.

3. Take some time to celebrate the moments where you have taken action, solved problems, spoken up, and made things happen. Be proud of yourself for that strength!

CHAPTER 14

FROM HIDDEN TO SEEN

by May Simpson

*Ye are the light of the world. A city that is set
on a hill cannot be hid. Neither do men light
a candle, and put it under a bushel, but on a
candlestick; and it giveth light unto all that are
in the house.*

— Matthew 5:14-15 KJV

My light was not shining bright. I kept it under the bushel, behind the door, in the closet—anywhere but on a candlestick. In fact, I remained hidden in the shadows for decades.

I was born in Tiptonville, a small town in the northwest corner of Tennessee. I was the ninth child. When I came along, my oldest sibling was 20 and the youngest was 5. My mother's due date was the end of July, but on June 17 she began hemorrhaging. My dad rushed her to the local doctor, who had delivered all their other children.

With a worried look, he said, "Get her to the hospital."

It was 40 minutes away. By the time they arrived, my mom was in a critical state from the loss of blood. They started giving her transfusions; however, they quickly ran out of her rare blood type, so they had to bring it in from surrounding counties. They stopped the bleeding briefly, but when it started again, the doctors were forced to perform an emergency C-section to save us both. They were genuinely concerned about our chances for survival.

Complicating matters was that the doctors were convinced I would not survive without a blood transfusion due to our RH incompatibility: Dad's blood was positive, and my mother was RH negative. The antibodies made in the mother's body can cross the placenta and attack the baby's blood, which my parents knew because it had happened to their eighth child. He had died two days after his birth.

The doctors were adamant that I needed the blood transfusion. My mother prayed and didn't get peace about the procedure. She believed I would not survive it, so instead she prayed, "God, take her or heal her!"

And 62 years later, I'm still here.

It's a miraculous story, yet amazingly, I did not grow up in the spotlight in my family. Quite the opposite in fact: I grew up living in the shadows. I had hidden from the very beginning, since my struggle to survive being born.

We moved to Chicago when I was a baby. Around age 5, I came home one day to find our living room in disarray. A photo of my parents was shredded to pieces... glass was everywhere. My father had destroyed it.

As a kid, I had no clue what was wrong with my dad. I later learned he had PTSD from serving in World War II. My mom defended him, since she had known him prior to the war. He had been a song leader in our church and a God-fearing, family-oriented man.

Not long after this incident, we moved back to Tiptonville, where my dad continued to drink daily. When he was agitated, he would throw things like ashtrays or glasses. One evening, as my mother and I sat on the couch, he threw a glass pitcher full of tea against the wall behind us. Shards of glass flew everywhere. My mom kept her peace, but I was frightened, so I hid.

One time Dad threw a glass and accidently hit my sister. It broke his heart, so that was the last glass I ever saw him throw.

Although my dad never spanked me, I was afraid of him. He was not a physically abusive man—he was agitated inwardly, but it manifested in outbursts. I didn't understand how to discern this as a child. So I spent those years frightened and hid as much as I could.

During my teen years, I grew to love my dad. I really got to know him after spending nights watching war movies together and hearing about his days of service. We'd work in the garden, which I loved. I learned he was an incredible, family-loving man.

He passed away when I was 16. I was so glad we'd had those years together. Looking through the lens of a child, I saw an alcoholic dad who caused me to hide in fear. As an adult, I realized that my dad had self-medicated due to trauma suffered from the violence of war.

Although I ultimately had a good relationship with my dad before he passed away, my tendency to stay hidden was firmly rooted in my spirit.

I got very good at hiding over the years. I was very shy, timid, and quiet. But when I started singing at church at the age of 11 with my sisters in a gospel group, the doors began to open. Even as I allowed the gift of my voice to be heard, I still felt most comfortable standing behind my sisters in choir. And outside of that, I hid in the shadows and kept quiet, rarely speaking unless called upon.

Two months before I turned 18, I got married. I was married for 13 years. I really loved my husband and got comfortable in the relationship. During those years, my hiding skills were front and center. I avoided confrontations at all costs. I ultimately became so enmeshed with my husband that I became codependent. So I went on the road with him while he drove an 18-wheeler, drifting away from the gospel group and my church.

When I became a mother, I started to recognize my tendency to hide in the shadows. I didn't want that life for my children—I wanted them to be seen and heard. Continuing to hide wouldn't set a good example for them. I knew I needed to change.

My husband and I had different values and views on life. At the time, I was too caught up in his life to realize what was important in mine. We decided we were too different and that we would be better apart. He told me, "I love you and want you to find yourself and your happiness."

The divorce was devastating. I had been determined to be married for life, so I never saw it coming, even though I knew our relationship was not healthy. So I sought help from a counselor, who later referred me to a therapist.

It was then that I experienced my turning point—from hiding in the dark to finding my light. In our very first session, my therapist commented, "I see you as a hider—one who hides behind the door."

I was floored! How did he know?!

Over the next few months, we worked together. Eventually, I walked out of the shadows and stopped hiding. Healing followed, and finally I was set free.

When I came out from hiding, I began to find my voice and ultimately my genuine self—the one I had lost as a child.

I started to learn how to be true to who I am, how to say no to others when needed, and how to love and care for myself. I also learned to identify codependent triggers so that I would never go back into hiding.

Before I married my second husband, I shared my journey with him. He was very supportive and did not want me to go into hiding. Thirty-one years later, we are still together, and I am no longer hidden in the shadows. I am most proud of staying liberated while navigating a challenging blended family of six children. It feels so good to be free!

Throughout my jobs as a real estate agent, a flight attendant, an insurance agent, and a speaker, I proudly shined my light. And now as a coach, I empower others to come out from the shadows and shine theirs.

After I chose to no longer be hidden, people started telling me I was too loud. Someone actually said, "No one could be as happy as you—you just want to be heard!" I admit, when I found my voice, I might have gone a little overboard until I found a balance. I was just so happy to have a voice and to be seen and heard!

It would be lovely if that was the end of the story...that I came out from hiding, never to return. But life doesn't usually work that way.

In 2021, I was fiercely tested. I lost two of my sisters back-to-back, one from COVID and one due to a tragic car accident. Because I didn't know how to cope with such enormous losses, my instinctive reaction was to hide. That had been my coping mechanism for so many years.

Fortunately, I had tremendous mentors and coaches in my life at the time (and still do). God always knows what we need! They reminded me to give myself grace, follow the path I needed to heal, and take the necessary time to recover. With their guidance, and by leaning on my faith, I did not and could not stay hidden for long. My light continued to shine in the midst of one of the greatest storms of my life.

As an Unstoppable Influencer, it's my responsibility and honor to be unapologetically ME and to stay free no matter what adversity comes my way. I now know that I was born to be SEEN so that I can help others uncover and shine their light in the world. I believe that I was born for such a time as this, and so are you.

KEY TAKEAWAYS

✦ Labels instilled in us as children can become firmly stuck on us well into adulthood. Removing those false labels can take some time. Leaning on the experiences of professionals and the Word of God are two great resources.

✦ Even the most stubborn of labels can be removed.

✦ We don't always know what's going on beneath the surface when it comes to others, so we mustn't judge. Always show compassion and grace.

✦ If you have been hiding, codependent, or a victim of abuse, seek professional help. There is HOPE for you, and you can be free from the pain of your past.

✦ Your light and your voice are needed in the world. You were designed to be seen and heard. You are valuable.

FREE YOURSELF

1. Recognize where in your life you are hiding or where you feel you are a victim. Take notice of whether you are in an unhealthy, codependent relationship.

2. Once you uncover areas where you feel you are hiding or trapped, find a safe mentor, a therapist, a coach, or a like-minded support group. Connect with them to get the support and accountability you need.

3. Speak up! Use your voice. You matter, and others need to hear your story so they too can be free to be their true authentic selves.

CHAPTER 15

FROM FAILURE TO INFINITE POTENTIAL

by Misty Lyon

*Courage allows the successful woman to fail—
and to learn powerful lessons from the failure—
so that in the end, she didn't fail at all.*

— **Maya Angelou**

Do you remember as a child being asked what you wanted to be when you grew up? For my brother and me, the answers were never the same. Everything from veterinarian to soldier to ballerina to cowboy. This is a blessing that most children seem to have innately—the ability to see infinite opportunities.

But at some point, I started to lose the ability to see the possibilities. Before I knew it, I was 40 years old, and I felt like I was in *Groundhog Day*. In that movie, every time Bill Murray wakes up, it's always Groundhog Day. Each day is the same as the previous one. My life: work, motherhood, eat, sleep, repeat. This "hamster wheel of life" was so unexciting compared to what I had dreamed of as a child.

At 40, I still didn't know what I wanted to be. My job was just a job. I felt like such a loser because I seemed to float like a butterfly from one job to the next with no direction. I'd worn so many hats during my working career of 10+ jobs. However, I wasn't happy. I was blessed to have a job, yet I felt like a failure because I didn't do work that was truly fulfilling. And that wasn't the only place I felt that way—I frequently felt I was failing as a mom as well.

Ever since my son was born, it has been just the two of us. He sees his dad every other weekend (due to distance) and every other week during the summer. Our daily world is literally just the two of us and Grandma, who fortunately lives right across the street. While we have some friends too, our nucleus is small.

The lack of community and connection for my son was evident in our day-to-day dynamics. We had many arguments. Although some were par for the course when raising a child, I knew that many of them were due to not having the right tools or enough support. My son told me more than once that as soon as he was able to, he would leave home—and me—and that I would be lucky to see him on holidays.

Although these words were from an upset child not getting his way, they stung. I took them as proof that I was failing as a mother. And as if my perceived failures in my job and as a mother weren't enough, I was convinced I was a failure in God's eyes as well.

When I became pregnant out of wedlock, there was an unfortunate series of events involving some members of my super-conservative church. The turmoil that ensued, including real and perceived judgment, led me to a very dark place regarding my relationship with Christ. I didn't know how to get back to having a solid relationship with Him.

In short, I felt like a failure in multiple areas, and I wore that label for far too long.

During this period, my health began to suffer, so I joined a weight-loss community. The community leader recommended a book called *Unstoppable Influence* and shared how it had helped her grow and become successful.

Little did I know that my journey was about to change course. Groundhog Day was finally over! It was time to remove my false I'm a failure label and put on my truth label: I have infinite potential!

Here's what happened…

I joined my first Unstoppable Influence 21-day challenge, which helped me realize that the connection between me and God was the key to tapping into my potential and bringing to life all the possibilities I had dreamed of as a child.

Since joining the Unstoppable Influence community and starting my own growth journey, I have discovered many wonderful tools to bridge the gap from where I was to where I wanted to go in realizing my purpose.

I combined a few of my favorites into one tool—WNS, which is an acronym for God Winks, Nudges, and Smacks. It helped me to stop worrying about failure and to instead become more courageous because I know I'm not alone.

God is with me…giving me Winks, Nudges, and Smacks along the way.

As Maya Angelou said: "Courage allows the successful woman to fail—and to learn powerful lessons from the failure—so that in the end, she didn't fail at all."

If I see WNS and trust what God is trying to tell me, I cannot fail; I can only grow.

Does this guarantee a favorable outcome? Of course not. But if I choose to take action on the WNS, I'm tapping into a sea of infinite potential and can learn valuable lessons that can also help me serve others along the way. It's the ultimate win-win!

My own growth journey has been filled with WNS along the way. Are you ready to learn how WNS is at play in your life?

The W stands for a God **Wink**, which is something that can seem like a coincidence, but if you're looking, you can see the divine at play.

The N stands for a God **Nudge**, which is more than a coincidence. It's like when you know something or you feel compelled to do something, but you don't know WHY or HOW. You just KNOW you must do it, even if it's scary.

The S is for God **Smacks**. These are the moments in your life where your world has just rocked you to your core. By the time that happens, you cannot NOT be aware of the change, and there is no going back to what your life used to be.

WNS shows up in a variety of ways, but one thing you should know is that they get louder the longer you don't listen. Oprah Winfrey describes this best. "The universe speaks to us constantly, but subtly at first. Will you heed the message before the whispers become a 'brick upside your head'?" The Winks are the whispers, and the brick upside the head is a God Smack.

From the beginning of my personal growth journey, God Winks were present. It was no coincidence my cousin-in-law was from the same tiny town as the weight-loss leader. And it was no coincidence that I found the path from the weight-loss community to the Unstoppable Influence community, where I found my tribe.

One God Nudge I experienced came via Facebook. I normally only post the required school pictures for family and maybe a random meme here and there. The rest of the time, I just scroll through everyone else's posts. But one day, I came across a video of a woman in a convertible with its top down, expressing her gratitude for life. She was just radiating pure joy, and I instantly wanted to be with her to experience it as well. Although we had never met, and it went against my typical Facebook protocol, I commented on her video.

Exactly one year later TO THE DAY, we were both on a plane to a retreat, where we discovered we were soul sisters. There are so many things we have in common—it's weird, yet AMAZING!

One week after I had finished collecting all the expenses for joining the Unstoppable Influence Inner Circle and paid for the program (I took out a loan), I found out that my job was ending. God Smack! I'm fairly laid-back, yet as a single mom finding out my job was ending, I heard all kinds of freak-out warning bells.

But by the next day, I began to see God at work. This job loss was a challenge but also an opportunity for me to surrender. I knew there had to be a reason for His timing, I just couldn't see it...yet.

One week later, I got a call telling me to apply for a specific job because they thought I would be a perfect fit. I applied, interviewed, and got the job. My old job was even extended a week so I wouldn't miss any work. The cherry on top was a pay increase...which was the exact same amount as the price I had just paid for my Inner Circle membership!

These little Winks, Nudges, and Smacks have reminded me that even when I fail, I'm not alone. Also, that the "failures" are actually lessons that help me to tap into my infinite potential.

They are doing the same in your life. If you just open your eyes to the Winks, Nudges, and Smacks happening around you, you will open the door to your own amazing journey of infinite potential and growth!

KEY TAKEAWAYS

✦ The childlike possibilities you used to experience never went away; you just need to relearn how to see them.

✦ You are never alone, no matter how you may feel right now.

✦ WNS—Winks, Nudges, and Smacks—is a tool to remember God's way of showing you that you're not alone and that possibilities exist for you.

✦ Surrender to the fact you're human and at times you will feel like a failure, but you're NOT. Your "failure" is merely an opportunity for you to grow.

FREE YOURSELF

Expand your mindset so you can see all the possibilities—look for the God Winks in your life. An easy place to start is to look for one heart every day for 30 days. It can be anything: a leaf in your path, a painted rock, a picture from your kiddo, even an emoji someone sent you. Take a picture or note it in a journal so when things get hard you have it as a reminder of His love. Every time you acknowledge "This is the heart of the day!" know that it is a God Wink, showing you the possibilities are endless.

CHAPTER 16

FROM INDECISIVE TO CONFIDENT

by Ruth Reynolds Smith

We must have perseverance and, above all,
confidence in ourselves. We must believe that we
are gifted for something, and that this thing, at
whatever cost, must be attained.

— **Marie Curie**

Indecision—my Achilles' heel, my nemesis, a previously inescapable agent of my downfall. I have often felt delayed or tripped up by indecisiveness. Many times I have waited—paralyzed, unable to make a decision—and missed an opportunity. Sometimes I knew what I wanted to choose, but I hesitated wondering what other people might think of my choice.

For years, I hesitated to make decisions. According to an article in the *Wall Street Journal*, the average person makes over 35,000 decisions each day. I'd do fine with 34,975 of them, but for the remaining 25, it was challenging to make a final choice.

Initially, I really wanted to please my parents, my older siblings, my teachers, and friends. I wanted to be liked and to receive approval. The bulk of my decisions were based on guessing what other people wanted. I'd theorize, vainly trying to predict other people's potential satisfaction levels.

In third grade, I started working to master written music by taking beginner's piano lessons and singing. Each composer clearly conveyed what they wanted, but my novice fingers and vocal cords would not always cooperate. I tried to work directly from the music, but at times my technical ability took the notes on a slightly different path. The gap between written notes and what came out of my fingers or throat, even though based on my flawed thinking and/or execution, played into my sense of indecisiveness.

All those years of attempting to perform music precisely made me resistant to playing or singing in my own style. I *wanted* to just perform without music, but it was foreign territory.

As a college student, I took an improvisation class, hoping to break through. As it turned out, I was too rigid and bound to written notes. So I simply labeled myself as inept, rather than giving myself grace because it was something I hadn't learned yet. The improv class was a part of a gradual, unconscious tearing down of my self-confidence.

During early married life with an argumentative husband, my hesitation to make decisions grew stronger. I'd never lived with someone who argued, so I had no debating tools. I did not want to distress him to the point where he would explode, but unfortunately for me, what set him off varied daily. The same choice could be a good one one day and a bad one the next. That daily walk through the landmine of choices that may or may not cause an explosion eroded my confidence, leading to more indecisiveness and my "decidophobia."

We truly wanted children, but their arrival was partially a misplaced effort to improve our relationship. Being out of sync with each other as parents complicated critical decision-making.

(It is *so* important to make wise parental choices, especially for dependent wee ones. Parents' choices heavily impact children's lives, their well-being, and their sense of safety and love.)

Fifteen years into the marriage, I was faced with a major decision. After years of repeatedly weighing the pros and cons, including multiple joint sessions with various marriage counselors, I made a huge decision—to move away with my children. They were eight and ten years old at the time. I had agonized over all the possible ramifications. My deteriorated confidence made the choice even harder to define, plan, and execute.

Through the Lord's strength, the prayers and support of our out-of-state family, and friends who physically helped us move, we made that 100-mile relocation.

That move was a turning point. We had a new community, school, and workplace. My confidence level had been pretty strong with my former job, and the new one had several similarities. I was comfortable in my work world. I could serve people well through my skills and dedication. My new coworkers helped rebuild my self-confidence. I started relearning what it meant to be me, finally appreciating my strengths.

We were blessed with a good neighborhood and many friends. We had the freedom to decide what activities to include in our lives: visits to the zoo, camping, skating, adding cats to keep our dog company, and continuing our music. (Both children learned to play instruments, plus we all enjoyed singing.)

Many parts of our lives were quite idyllic. Yet I still felt wishy-washy. I was indecisive at critical junctures as a single parent in our day-to-day activities, such as setting rules for my children and holding firm boundaries for their sakes and for the harmony of our home.

As a single parent, so many routine decisions bogged me down.

+ Can they go to a friend's house?

+ Can we afford the registration fee for youth sports or clubs?

+ What will happen if they dye their hair? What if they don't? (*They* were sure they would be social outcasts.)

+ Who can we trust?

+ What meals will we eat this week?

In 2008, Kristina Guo published the DECIDE model of decision-making, including six parts:

+ **D**efine the problem.

+ **E**stablish (or **E**numerate/list) all the criteria and constraints.

+ **C**onsider (or **C**ollect) all the alternatives.

+ **I**dentify the best option.

+ **D**evelop and implement a plan of action.

+ **E**valuate/monitor the solution, and **E**xamine feedback.

My trusted mentor, Natasha Hazlett, teaches this:

> The meaning of the word *decide* comes from the Latin word *decidere*, which is a combination of two words: *de* means OFF and *caedere* means CUT. To decide literally means to CUT OFF. You make a decision and cut off the other "outs" so you'll move forward.

We don't have to see or understand the full picture to know what the next step is. We take that and then look for the following one. When you break any action down step-by-step, each individual step is not complicated. My confidence level could have been much higher and my decisiveness much improved years ago if I hadn't always wanted to know the complete picture or "how" something would come to fruition. Stepping out *in faith*, then reviewing the results and continuing to move forward is key.

When making decisions now, I like to consider the 4 Ts:

> **Tired:** I make the best decisions when well-rested. A good night's sleep helps me maintain focus and clarity throughout the day.
>
> **Timing:** I consider the timing of any particular decision. Perhaps it needs to wait, or I need to do further research.

Territory: I need to check whether a decision is in my zone of responsibility or someone else's.

Truth: It is most important to see and sense God's guidance. Our Heavenly Father wants us to turn to Him. He cares about our outcomes. He's given us the Bible as guidance and direction. The Lord is Truth. We need to lean into His instruction and nudges. When we take action based on His input, it will greatly improve our output!

> *"Show me your ways, oh Lord; teach me your paths."*
> **— Psalm 25:4**

We do not have to carry everything on our own. I surround myself with positive women who are growing, learning, and seeking to improve their lives. As a bonus, their activities and goals line up with things I'm working on. Many of us connected through Unstoppable Influence. We keep things positive. We support one another through celebrations and sorrows. We strengthen each other's journeys.

These resilient, growth-minded women provide optimism, accountability, and input that helps me reach confident decisions when my own analysis feels limited or causes me to freeze up. Our connections have blossomed into friendships, stretched me to try new adventures, brought me more instruction and training, and helped illuminate my new career path.

Each day, I understand more fully the importance of taking confident action. My action to move years ago eventually led to my current marriage to my wonderful husband of 20+ years, three happily married adult children, their adored spouses, five precious grandchildren, and a great career. My increased confidence has propelled me to establish a website for my writing and coaching services. I've nearly completed my book. That once tentative, wavering woman from 25 years ago is now flourishing.

Please don't wait to take bold, confident action in the direction of your dreams. Being decisive allows you to be true to yourself and to be your best for those you love. Making decisions can be tough, but you have more strength and wisdom than you may think. Step forward boldly. It can change your life.

As a friend once told me, "This is not a dress rehearsal. This is your life!"

KEY TAKEAWAYS

✦ You will always have a multitude of options (35,000+ per day). You may not be certain that you are making the best decision, BUT it all starts with making an initial one.

✦ As you make a choice (*decidere*), the other options go away, and you gain clarity. Decisions can be adjusted.

✦ Embracing the joy of making solid decisions helps your confidence reach new heights and allows you to be your best for those around you. Enjoy the journey.

✦ You don't need to be what others want you to be. You have the freedom to be true to yourself!

FREE YOURSELF

1. Recognize the decisions you are feeling hesitant about. Take notice of what is holding you back. Make your wisest determination as to what will bring a positive outcome.

2. Choose one area of indecision and focus on that first. Move into action then adjust one step, one action at a time.

3. The next time you have a decision to make, run it through the DECIDE model and the 4 Ts (Tired, Timing, Territory, Truth).

4. Find positive ways to have a brighter outlook and lifted spirit, such as identifying and connecting with a support team that "gets you," then walk alongside each other through life.

CHAPTER 17

FROM I SHOULD TO I COULD

by Becky Wallery

*The only person you are destined to become is
the person you decide to be.*

— Ralph Waldo Emerson

As a little girl, I never knew what I should be when I grew up. I was fairly shy and a people pleaser. I wanted people to like me, and I wanted to be like other people. It confused me about what I wanted in my own life.

I longed so badly for someone to tell me what I should do, always looking for answers outside of myself as to what my next steps "should" be or how I "should" act. I never understood how other kids were so clear on what they wanted. I kept waiting for someone to tell me, "Becky, you should be this..."

In elementary school, I dreaded career week each year because I knew that by the end of the week they would want us to name our future career. Are you kidding me? I was just a kid! What did I know?

One year, I asked my friend her thoughts. She recommended that I be a baker.

(As a side note, my maiden name was Baker, and because I didn't have a better idea, I decided that this career choice would work for the time being.)

Becky Baker, the baker.

I wore a white baker's hat as I waited in line to tell everyone my career. My friend skipped around and sang, "Becky Baker, the baker!" and my face turned bright red. I couldn't believe I hadn't been able to come up with something better.

Fast-forward to high school, when kids typically become clearer on what they wanted to study in college or elsewhere. I loved to travel, so being a flight attendant seemed like the perfect opportunity for me.

That is, until I actually flew for the first time.

It was a school trip to California, and my head and stomach hurt the entire flight. My dreams of becoming a flight attendant quickly faded.

So when I graduated, I headed to college as "undecided."

How did I end up in college still not knowing what I wanted to be?

Why did I even go to college in the first place?

My first academic advisor asked me if I was there to get the "MRS" degree. Seriously?! No, I wasn't attending college solely to find someone to marry. The reason I was there had to do with the example my mom had set years earlier.

When I was 10, my dad had a health scare and ended up in the hospital. I didn't realize it at the time, but my parents were worried that something even more serious would happen to him. So they decided that my mom would go back to college so she could support my brother and me if something serious did happen.

My mom was inspiring to watch as she balanced school, work, and family life. Occasionally, she would ask me to help her with a math assignment or an art project that she didn't enjoy. I know that she struggled with this change happening so late in her life, although I never once heard her complain about it.

I didn't want to struggle later in life like my mom had, so I decided I should attend college, even though I had no clue what to study. Although I started off as "undecided," my first computer class was so enjoyable that I ended up majoring in computer science and eventually became a software engineer.

With that, I had done what I thought I "should" — complete college and find a career. Check!

Because family was so important to me growing up, and I loved traveling to see relatives, another belief became ingrained within me: that I "should" get married and have a family.

So one month after graduating from college, I got married and started my career. I checked off yet another box of what I thought a person "should" do with their life.

After being married for a few years, kids came next on the list. I now have the privilege of being a mom to a wonderful son and twin daughters. Being Mom is not something I would ever change. My family has been a huge joy in my life.

So everything should have been perfect by then, right? After all, I had checked all the boxes. Yet I felt like something was still missing.

As I continued down the path of what I believed life "should" look like, I still didn't truly know who I was or what I wanted.

The reality was that I had lost myself.

I started to live life on autopilot, just making it through each day only to have to repeat it the next...and the next...and the next. I greatly anticipated the day when I had worked hard enough that I could reach the coveted prize of retirement, and finally "live freely and truly enjoy life."

Then within a span of two years, I lost what I thought was my dream job and I lost both of my parents.

It was like a bomb had been dropped on my life. And it was a massive wake-up call. I didn't want to spend the next 25 years working at a corporate job only to die without truly living my dream life. Enough was enough!

I knew I had to find something to break me out of my routine and set me on a new path. This desire sent me searching for something to help me start dreaming again and unbury me from all of the beliefs and "shoulds" that I felt pressure to conform to.

I wanted to ditch the "shoulds" and start imagining what life "could" look like.

I wanted to dream bigger and co-create the life I desired.

It was time to open my eyes to the potential opportunities the world had to offer. Being so caught up in pursuing what I thought I "should" do, I was unaware of what was out there waiting for me. I wanted to open my heart and mind to something bigger than myself and be willing to learn about things that were new, different, and out of my comfort zone, even if I didn't have all the answers yet.

My awakening led me to join a network marketing company. It wasn't what I had been looking for—to be honest, direct sales was the furthest thing from my mind. But I could see in those ladies a desire for something more in their lives. I was drawn to their excitement, their motivation, and their passion for freedom with their time and their lives.

Within that business, I discovered personal development, and I started to expand my mind to the possibilities of what **could be**.

I started to dream bigger for myself and my family. I was open to new ideas and teachings that I would have been closed off to in the past because they didn't fit into my beliefs.

Could I be a speaker on a stage? Why not?

Could I write a book? Yes!

Could I retire early from a corporate career and still enjoy the life I desired? Others have done it, so why couldn't I?

Could I have good relationships and a better connection with my own spirituality, and could I love myself more? YES, YES, AND YES!

With a fresh perspective, I headed down my new path.

One of the most important mindset shifts I made after this transformation from "I should" to "I could" was becoming more open-minded.

Previously, ideas or beliefs that I hadn't grown up with were scary. What if I was judged for believing or even learning about something that others didn't believe in?

I began learning how to discern things for myself and use my intuition to know what felt right. I adjusted and adopted my own beliefs to what I really believed, not what others thought I should.

I also stopped judging others for things I didn't understand. While I don't necessarily agree with everything that everyone says or does, I now look at the world with curiosity to try to understand each person's view of the world.

This was my second major mindset shift that had a meaningful impact in my life. We were not put on this Earth to live a mediocre life or simply exist.

I encourage you to truly look around at this amazing world we live in. The beauty that exists all around you. When you look at how each little detail was designed, you have to know there is something greater than us that has orchestrated this masterpiece.

Were we meant to live a life that we are not happy with? I say, "No!" We are meant to live a life where we can all dream bigger than we even thought was possible!

Friend, we live in an abundant world, and the desires we are given are ours for a reason. You are not required to settle for a life that doesn't align with YOUR dreams and YOUR desires.

Let's all go out and live the life we COULD instead of living within the bounds of what we or others feel that we SHOULD. In doing so, you could experience more freedom and happiness than you've ever imagined.

KEY TAKEAWAYS

✦ Life is not about what you *should* be doing. It's about all of the possibilities that *could* be.

✦ Be open to options outside your normal beliefs. Our beliefs are not set in stone: they can change.

✦ Dream so much bigger than you thought possible. When you get there, dream even bigger.

FREE YOURSELF

1. Is anyone projecting their thoughts, opinions, or beliefs onto you? Be curious about whether they are your own thoughts, opinions, or beliefs or just something you took on.

2. Do you have any "should" or "should not" statements impacting the direction of your life in a way that you do not want? What could you believe instead that better aligns with your own beliefs?

3. Dream bigger! List all the things you could be, do, or have in your life.

CHAPTER 18

FROM RESTRAINED TO UNLEASHED

by Cassandra Lennox

*Today you are You, that is truer than true. There
is no one alive who is Youer than You.*

— Dr. Seuss (Theodor Seuss Geisel)

I can still envision my scared and determined little
eight-year-old self and the stack of notebooks on my
bedroom desk—and the emotional journey they represented.

Each notebook was filled with childlike scribbles from
colorful gel pens, misspelled words and uneven rhymes,
and my heart and soul poured out onto the pages. I frequently wrote inspirational poems about trying again
or being a friend and spelling out my fears of others
disliking me. My quiet and insecure self found refuge
in those pages.

Little Me spent hours in my room, jotting down
thoughts. The hardships of youth were temporarily

calmed by my hours of solitude with a pencil and paper. Those words were there just for me, hidden in the desk drawers when friends would come over to play and put back in their spot upon the desk after their parents picked them up.

The rhymes, quotes, and stories were a part of me that I very carefully hid from the world for several years.

If others knew that the one thing I was really good at, my special skill that I indulged in and was practically my lifeline, was rhyming...

What would they say?

What would they think?

I was certain that I'd get made fun of even *more* than I already did, and I was already at my limit. Plenty of things about me were easy to make fun of, apparently. I was short, over-emotional, and hard of hearing, just to name a few.

I felt that I needed to hide who I was, just so I could fit in. Being "different" felt like a weakness, and in my need to feel accepted, that was not an option.

The "what ifs" of exposing the real me (especially my writing) were so crippling that I even wrote poems about *them*!

I wrote about nearly everything in my life, for years. I truly doubt a single day passed without writing. I was in my own emotional box, restrained by my insecurities, doubts, fears, and incessant negative self-talk, which chattered in my head almost nonstop...except when I was writing.

It was the release I needed. My thoughts settled when I poured them onto the page, and I felt most alive in those moments.

From time to time, bit by bit, I'd allow others to glimpse at my writing, allowing them to see the real me. The very first was a friend who came to my house. (That time was unintentional—she found my notebook!)

One time, I entered a talent competition, where I recited an original poem. Ironically, it was the one I had written years earlier at the request of my friend who had found the notebook!

Around the same time, I shared a poem on my high school stage that was a tribute to the senior class. Years later, after reading a few of my favorite works, some of my friends commented, "This is exactly how I feel, and you put it to words." Not long after that, I got the nudge to compile my writings from over the years into my first published book!

And that was when the emotions terrifying, beautiful, nauseating, and empowering all collided. It was a significant milestone. I felt a little less restrained. More vulnerable, yes, but that comes with the territory.

Over the next several years, I published four more books, which included a lot of rhymes, my wild imagination and quirkiness, and my poetic uniqueness.

Through it all, I was still afraid and uncertain and desperately sought shadows to hide in.

In 2021, I felt more exposed than ever. I had just released a book that represented my journey over the previous 18 years. I had poured everything I had into it. And although it was focused on my "unleashing" and the pivotal steps I took on my journey, I included everything that I knew others might laugh at or ridicule.

Knowing that the words were now available to anyone and everyone, I couldn't help but wonder what Little Me would think…

Would she be scared for me? Worried and anxious?

Or would she jump for joy, recalling how she had proudly declared, "I'm going to be an author someday"?

I decided to trust that there was a genuine and significant reason that I felt a rush of happiness and peace every time I heard that my words helped, inspired, or resonated with someone. Especially when it was all in rhyme or deeply vulnerable or me being "Cassie outside the box."

I'll never forget the day I was contacted by an old high school classmate. I had never thought she liked me very much. But in her message, she told me what my book meant to her. She had purchased it just to support me, since she had known me growing up. But it ended up being the "best book [she'd] ever read." She told me how much she appreciated it, how deeply it resonated, and how it helped her through a certain period in her life.

Her gratitude ignited a realization in me.

My entire life, I had been so worried about the negative things people would say instead of focusing on the positive impact I could make.

I reflected on all the negativity I had heard from people, including comments that my writing "would never be anything more than a hobby," being laughed at for my childlike ways, and for overachieving when it came to writing.

There was so much negativity associated with what I believed to be one of the strongest gifts and basis for who I AM. But why did I take it to heart?

I realized that I had allowed my gift and my truth to be overshadowed and dimmed by how others felt about it, or how I feared they'd feel, when I had truly made up those assumptions in my own head!

I wasn't placing the weight on how *I myself felt about my words*. I'd placed the balance of the scale over what *others* thought, or what I *assumed* they would think.

So in that moment of realization, I chose to tip the scale from restrained to unleashed. I'd write whatever I felt. I'd let it all out. And I'd share it with the world.

The gratitude and excitement, the release and uplifting feeling of lightness and peace after letting my words out, the childlike giddiness when the rhyme flowed beautifully, like it was just meant to be...

They allowed me to feel that I am right where I belong and oftentimes genuinely happy.

I had held back for years, robbing myself of *my* greatest joy in life...simply because it wasn't someone else's and I assumed they'd think negatively.

And because of this, I wasn't the only one being robbed of it. I was stealing that joy—that peace, comfort, laughter, connection, and encouragement—from any and all who could benefit from my words.

Our words help no one if we take them with us to the grave. Rather, we have a beautiful opportunity to let them out into the world.

Now, I proudly allowed what others claimed to be my "silly, childish talent" to be my strength and a momentous aspect of my career and the legacy I am creating.

I share often, and I even sometimes kick my comfort zone to the curb. I am vulnerable, often without shame or anxiety. I challenge myself to level up my writing and find ways to combine my skills and joy around helping others on their journeys.

The decision to unleash my words has allowed others to do the same. I have helped many women tell their stories, embrace their strengths and experiences, and create a beautiful ripple effect.

I recognize and truly believe that what makes us different makes us unique, which in turn makes us responsible to share that gift with the world. Because that's what it is—a gift. Gifts are meant to be shared, enjoyed, reciprocated, and used to create memories.

If I had understood earlier that my talents I had thought were laughable could also be life-changing, perhaps I could have shared more of my writing sooner.

Friend, whatever talents, passions, or gifts you possess, I hope my story inspires you to reframe your limiting thoughts and others' opinions so you can chase your dreams.

If you feel restrained right now, know that you can break free because the power and strength are within you. And the world is awaiting the awesomeness you will unleash!

KEY TAKEAWAYS

✦ Instead of spending years worrying about what others think, or what you think they think, look inward to how *you* feel about things. It's your life and your talents, not theirs.

✦ Oftentimes we put restrictions on ourselves yet blame others. It comes back to a conscious decision to break down the barriers, whether real or imagined.

✦ There is no one exactly like you, and that is a gift. Your differences should be celebrated. You were born to unleash everything you truly are.

FREE YOURSELF

1. Write down what makes you unique and brings you joy.

2. Take a good look at your greatest skills, qualities, characteristics that make you YOU.

3. If any trigger thoughts of negative comments, remind yourself of the value of your uniqueness.

4. Complete this phrase. "If I _____, then I can _____ and unleash who I am and what I am meant to be in the world!"

CHAPTER 19

FROM TIMID TO BOLD

By Erin Gardiner

Be bold and mighty forces will come to your aid.

— Basil King

When I was younger, I wouldn't speak to other people much at all. Even as an adult, I have found myself in situations where I wanted to say something, either with a person or in a group, and felt I couldn't. I was afraid to ask for help or support.

Not surprisingly, I'm an introvert by nature. I prefer time alone or in small groups of people. Large social gatherings are not my favorite, nor is speaking in public.

As if being an introvert wasn't enough, I was also extremely timid. I was quiet and reserved and tried my best to hide in the corner. I felt like everyone was staring at me because I didn't fit in. And if I could have disappeared, I would have.

If I needed to figure out how to get somewhere, would I ask for directions? Never! Would I dare go to a party where I barely knew anyone and just go and talk to someone new? Nope!

High school is typically the place where students start dating and going out to parties, but for me that never happened. I spent my time alone, at home in my room. I didn't attend my school's Welcome Week activities other than to be matched with a guiding senior (only to never see her again).

On occasion, I attended social events with friends, but mostly I avoided anything that involved big crowds or new people. I had a few friends, but we lost touch soon after graduation, in part because I didn't reach out to them.

I lived within walking distance of my high school, so at lunchtime I went home because I wasn't comfortable eating in the cafeteria with everyone else. I had a few classmates to sit with if I had to stay at school for some reason, but I preferred eating by myself at home.

One day, I was leaving to walk home for lunch and walked past a guy I knew. He said, "Hi," but all I could do in response was give him a small smile. As I continued walking, a couple of girls said loudly, "Wow, she can't even say 'hi' back!"

I was so embarrassed; I kept walking and did not look back. After this, I dreaded encountering them again. I started using the back stairwell rather than feel the embarrassment again.

I wanted to be liked, have lots of friends, and even have a boyfriend, but I was too timid to do anything about it.

How did I get here? When I was younger, I was somewhat comical and relaxed around my family, but I wasn't that way around others. But around age 12, I experienced physical and emotional abuse. This made me extremely self-conscious, so I lacked confidence and was unwilling to express myself publicly. So I spent most of my free time at home...which unfortunately meant even more frequent encounters with the person who filled my head with nasty thoughts.

I did tell others about the abuse, but because they hadn't seen it happen, they didn't believe me.

This caused a chain reaction: I became highly upset that nobody believed me, to the point that I was sent to anger management classes. I couldn't believe it. I thought, *Why am I the one being sent to anger management classes? I'm not the one with anger issues!*

I became even more withdrawn. I believed there was no point in speaking about my concerns, thoughts, or feelings with anyone because they wouldn't listen anyway. Eventually, my parents realized what was going on, but by then I had started university and my abuser no longer lived in the house.

However, the damage had been done.

At university, I didn't attend many functions. When I did, I sat alone, avoiding eye contact so people would leave me alone. I wished that I could be like the popular students: outgoing and members of all the social committees. But I wasn't like them. I had decided that I was timid, shy, and definitely not gregarious.

One time, I was given some university assignments that required group work and presentations. I wasn't happy about it because I was forced to interact more with others. So I did the bare minimum, just enough to pass the class.

It wasn't until my third year in university that I finally got involved in something meaningful that resulted in a life-changing shift. I had heard about a student-run work-abroad organization. I was intrigued, so I signed up for the informational meeting.

At the meeting, we learned more about the organization, and I was added to a smaller group to meet regularly. I enjoy traveling and learning about other cultures, so having a work-abroad opportunity was very enticing. Although I didn't work in a different country myself, I was participating in a small group and contributed to several students coming to work in Canada. I had finally started to come out of my protective shell.

After university, I spent two and a half months in Europe. Part of my trip was spent with a couple of friends; the other part, I traveled alone.

This is where the magic happened.

Traveling solo around Europe might not be everyone's solution to timidness, but it worked like a charm for me. It's pretty much impossible to be timid in a foreign city while alone, looking for a place to spend the night when all the hostels are full.

On one occasion, I even stayed in a random stranger's living room! Yes, the girl who had walked home for lunch every day as a child to avoid being around people. True story!

When I arrived by train in Sweden, the station was completely full. After discovering that there were no hostels or hotels available, I was pretty upset. A man approached me and offered a bed in his apartment living room. (Two others also went with him.) As a young woman traveling alone, this could have turned out poorly, but fortunately I made it through, and it was a great experience. I ended up with not only a place to sleep but also a whole room to myself!

After graduation, I participated in numerous organizations and direct-sales companies that have also helped me to overcome my timidity. For me, direct sales helped me stretch. I was forced to talk to lots of people I didn't know.

I discovered that it's easier to attend a trade show and discuss products with people I didn't know than to reach out to people I already know. Anytime I approached a family member, I always worried that they would get mad and hate me.

When I talked to a stranger at a trade show, they could say no, but the chance of me seeing them again (or them remembering me later) was small. That thought made me bolder, so I soon had no issues talking with people I didn't know.

I now regularly have random conversations at stores. As an empath, I am a great listener, and people naturally gravitate toward me. However, being empathic means I tend to take on other people's feelings so my body and brain believe that they are my own, which can be draining.

The desire to learn more about myself led me to Unstoppable Influence. In the fall of 2018, I took the biggest leap of faith of my life—I traveled solo from Canada to Salt Lake City, Utah, to a conference where I didn't know a soul! I'd talked with some people on social media, but I had not met anyone personally.

I took the bold leap to attend, on pure faith that it would be good for me. I even shared a room with two attendees who were looking for a roommate. I was scared to death, but it was truly a life-altering experience.

I had proved to myself that I was BOLD.

I've worked at the same place for more than 20 years. When I started, I was given an office near the back of the building, which was a blessing because it allowed me time to get used to the people there. If I wanted to be alone, I could just retreat to my office.

But recently, one of my coworkers commented that he liked me better when I was quiet and didn't participate in the group banter. (Of course, he was the butt of the jokes that day.)

Have I completed my growth toward being my bold self? Of course not; it's a journey, not a destination.

But I have recognized that because I am an introvert (which carries its own set of strengths), I need to consciously push myself to go beyond my comfort zone. I am also seeing a therapist to learn how to speak my true thoughts and feelings aloud.

When I think back to those girls in high school, I imagine myself turning around and saying something clever. But then I realize they probably wouldn't have said anything in the first place because the bolder me would have said "Hi!" to that boy.

KEY TAKEAWAYS

✦ Being timid may be a subconscious protection mechanism that serves its purpose at a certain time, but to reach your full potential, you must take control of your life.

✦ Once given the opportunity to bloom, starting small within your comfort zone will give you the confidence to keep moving forward.

✦ Taking a chance on a bold decision can result in a large impact.

✦ Learning and growing never ends; to continue to grow, you must consciously push beyond your comfort zone daily.

FREE YOURSELF

1. Start small. You can't change anything overnight. For example, if you're timid like I was, start by purposely asking a store clerk where something is located or asking someone in the park what time it is.

2. Take advantage of opportunities to get together with friends and family often, and be yourself. Interacting with others in a social setting is a skill that can be learned, and it gets easier with practice.

3. Get help when you need it, and accept support from those around you. This could be meeting with a therapist who can help you through something that is holding you back, or accepting a friend's offer to look after your children for a couple hours so you can take time for yourself. Instead of saying, "No, thank you—I'm fine"…say, "Thank you," and graciously accept the offer of help.

CHAPTER 20

FROM I CAN'T TO I CAN

by Gina Faust

She believed she could, so she did.

— R.S. Grey

As a little girl, I had big dreams and a long bucket list.

As I was growing up, my biggest dream was to travel the world as a missionary helping those less fortunate, opening an international Missionaries of Charity foundation that would help feed and deliver medical help to people and places most in need.

I imagined that most of my time would be spent in Africa. I dreamed I would be an author, writing about the village people I had spent time with, sharing stories I learned about their culture and how they survived. I even fantasized about becoming an archeologist, making significant discoveries in Israel in all the places Jesus had walked. And I always felt that no matter what path I chose in life, I would be a talented guitar-playing singer!

However, as I grew up, the list became shorter and shorter because I was constantly told "You can't." Those two words became tightly sewn into my heart and mind.

I was told...

"You can't wear red undergarments. That is what girls who are not proper wear."

"You can't ride a dirt bike—that's just for boys."

"You can't try out for cheerleading because you aren't as good as the others."

"You can't date the boy with long hair. He's no good."

"You can't travel the world by yourself."

"You can't become an archeologist—you're not smart enough."

"You can't work at a preschool because that's not a real job."

Being told "You can't" became a daily occurrence.

I hid the pain and began making poor choices to purposely displease the person who had embedded "YOU CAN'T" inside of me. This was the beginning of losing my true self.

I remember the lump in my throat when I was 23 as I sat at the dinner table, telling my mom that I was pregnant. She slammed her plate down on the table and words of fire flew from her lips. "You are a DISGRACE to the family. You can't have a baby out of wedlock!" Her solution for the matter was abortion.

After many heated arguments and tears of pain, I was told that the only other way I could remain part of the family was to marry the father of my unborn child. But I would be unable to speak about the baby until well after the wedding. So that's what I did.

Years passed by, and the "YOU CAN'T"s escalated.

At one point, I contemplated leaving a highly abusive marriage with my four children. The response from my mom was as expected. She believed that I should stay married because there was no possible way I could support myself without a job.

My abusive husband told me, "You can't have a job." He also said that I couldn't leave him because no one would want a woman with four children.

Clearly a pattern was forming in my life. I went from one person telling me "You can't" to another!

By that point in my life, I was broken, lost, and scared. I began praying for God to help me find a solution and to protect me and my children from harm.

Two years of prayer led me to finding a slice of bravery, and I went to work at a preschool. The job provided insurance for my children. I was able to make some friends, began attending church functions, and eventually escaped the abusive marriage.

Finally, I had turned "I can't" into "I CAN."

But it wasn't all sunshine and rainbows. I didn't realize that the words I had been told for so long by multiple people were so deeply embedded in my soul.

It wasn't long before the person telling me "I can't" in nearly every circumstance was myself. Hearing that for so long had left me empty and afraid.

It became hard to make decisions on my own for fear it would be the wrong decision, and then I would hear *I told you that you couldn't do it.*

I didn't want to prove everyone right, so I became a recluse, staying home, the place I felt safe and unjudged, as much as possible. I was terrified to do anything for fear of failure. Dreaming was no longer something I felt comfortable doing. What was the point in dreaming if I knew that I couldn't bring my dreams to life?

After 15 years of raising my children and only joining in with others when absolutely necessary, I stepped way out of my comfort zone and attended a women's retreat.

Walking into the event, I was handed a small black bag with rocks in it, which I was asked to wear around my neck. The rocks represented any pain I was carrying inside me. When I felt ready to release the pain, I was told to put the bag of rocks at the foot of the cross.

I held on to that bag until the very last night, when I bravely set it at the foot of the cross, surrendering all my pain and fears to God.

I had been afraid to give it away because that would mean my life would change. I had lived with I CAN'T for so long, I didn't know whether or how I could change it to I CAN.

One year after leaving my I CAN'Ts at the cross, I reunited with my high school sweetheart. We got married, and I continued to struggle with allowing him to care for me and feeling comfortable being myself. His unconditional love was foreign to me.

Shortly after we were married, I finished my teaching degree, with his support. Each time I cried, "I can't!" he responded, "You can do it!"

This was the beginning of finding the true me again.

I *released* the pain and the label of "I can't" and began *believing* in myself. I *changed* my words to "I CAN." I saw a beautiful path unrolling. The hard part was accepting the path as a gift and believing that I was worthy of being loved and respected.

I was well into my forties by the time I took that first step onto my new path. Through social media, I connected with a childhood friend who I hadn't seen in 20 years. Over coffee, we reminisced about my desire to do mission work in Africa. I hadn't given much thought to my bucket list for years. She told me that her husband had been going to Africa for many years, taking mission teams with him.

After talking with my husband, meeting with hers, and getting a God Wink, I decided to go to Africa!

Though I said "YES" out loud and began planning for the trip, over the next several months, the "I CAN'T"s creeped in.

As I anticipated telling my mother about my travel plans, the all-too-familiar nervous feelings began to stir. Sure enough, when I told her, she immediately scowled. "You can't do that. You have to stay and take care of me. Are those people in Africa more important to you than I am?"

But I stood strong and didn't allow her words to affect me. I went on that mission trip to Africa, and then again two years later.

After my second mission trip, I had an epiphany. God spoke to me very clearly. "Feed my people."

This led me to leave the preschool where I had worked for more than 20 years. I started a food truck, despite my mom telling me, "You can't do that. You don't know anything about running a business."

I ignored her negative words with a fierce "YES, I CAN" attitude. I spoke with several restaurant and food truck owners, researched how to write a business plan, and started on a mission to serve those less fortunate.

A fellow food truck owner helped me find a truck. He found one at an unbelievably low listing price, especially given its excellent condition. Little did I know, this food truck was not for me at all but part of God's bigger plan. I operated it for two seasons, and then I felt it was time to move on.

Soon after, I received a message from a friend who was a full-time missionary in Africa asking about my food truck. Her budget was less than the asking price, however after much prayer, it was placed on my heart to sell it to her. She transported the food truck to Africa, where it remains today, continuing to serve God's people.

And it all started with "I can!" Once I began saying that, so many new doors opened up, and I found my purpose!

Believing "I can" led me to the Unstoppable Influence community, where I found amazing friends, personal and business growth opportunities, and new ways to step outside of my comfort zone!

Today, I am so grateful for every chance I get to say, "Yes, I CAN!"

If you find yourself saying "I can't" a lot, consider dropping your bag full of rocks and do the work to release past hurts so you can move to "I can!"

Believe in yourself. I believe in you!

KEY TAKEAWAYS

✦ Releasing negative labels opens room to believe in yourself, allowing you to change your words to "I can."

✦ Practicing self-compassion by loving and affirming yourself daily will help shield other people's negative words or energy from harming you. Do not define yourself based on what others think.

✦ Follow your dreams and the path that has been created especially for you. Don't give up believing in yourself; push through the hard times one baby step at a time. Surround yourself with others who will share in your dreams and tell you, "You can do it."

✦ Realizing that the only person holding you back is you could be the first step outside of your comfort zone, which can open doors to many opportunities.

✦ So many others are waiting for you to share your gifts and purpose. Don't make them wait any longer!

FREE YOURSELF

1. Journaling is a great way to release stress and connect with your inner needs and desires! Quiet your heart and spend some time doing this, using one or more of these prompts to get you started.

   - What are some ways that God has shown me His love?

   - Things I feel or have been told I can't do…

   - Things I can do….

   - My strengths are….

   - Write the top three things that bring you joy and why.

   - Make a bucket list filled with your dreams.

2. Make a commitment within the next 30 days to start shedding the I CAN'Ts.

3. Consider hiring a personal empowerment life coach who can help you create an action plan.

CHAPTER 21

FROM DIVORCED TO WHOLE

by Heather Romanski

*There are things in my life that are hard to rec-
oncile, like divorce. Sometimes it is very difficult
to make sense of how it could possibly happen.*

— Reese Witherspoon

I knew deep down that I should call off the wedding. I
knew I was in way over my head. But my parents had
spent so much money on invitations, a dress, and de-
posits. That was 1996, and by the spring of 2002, we
were divorced.

It's humorous now that I was so worried about my parents losing money and saving face that I went through
with a marriage that was destined for divorce.

Those five years of marriage were a mix of good and
bad, but that relationship was never one I would clas-
sify as solid or healthy. When I achieved success at the
office, there was no acknowledgement or celebration.
Instead, he would pepper me with questions.

"Don't you want more responsibility at work? Don't you want to make more money? Are you *really* satisfied working there?"

I was confident in my decision to leave, even though it meant moving back into my parents' house at the age of 29. Don't get me wrong, my parents are great people — loving, generous, and supportive. But who really wants to live in their parents' basement so close to 30?

By all appearances, I was happy to have a fresh start. In reality, I was a mess. The day we decided to get divorced, my soon-to-be-ex-husband had all but drained our savings account. I was horrified that I had been so trusting and naive.

I'm a smart woman. I have a bachelor's degree in computer science and business and a master's in business administration. Yet there I was — 29, broke, and alone.

I felt ashamed that I had allowed myself to be treated so badly. I was emotionally battered and broken. And to top it off, I was about to be *divorced*.

While the divorce was proceeding, things were really tense. We were fighting more than ever. We started therapy with the intention to save our marriage; however, a couple sessions in, we filed for divorce. While it didn't save my marriage, a year of counseling helped me rebuild my self-esteem and emotional well-being, setting me on a positive path forward.

My divorce was final in early 2002. By then, I had started catching up on some of the fun I had missed out on by marrying a man 14 years my senior. I took scuba diving lessons and then booked a trip to Honduras to put my new skills to use. My circle at the time was small but tight, and even though I had come out of the divorce with a mountain of debt, I had a fresh start.

In the summer of 2002, I was introduced to a guy named Paul at a mutual friend's birthday party. In early September, we went on our first date. He was kind, respectful, and quiet…so different from my first husband. He didn't have to be the center of every conversation, and he was genuinely interested in me and my work and activities. He was happy to socialize with my friends.

Best of all, he was patient and worked with me to slowly glue many of those broken pieces back together. When we met, I didn't even know who I was. My likes and dislikes had been formed around what I thought would appease my ex-husband. The divorce process was tenuous, but this new relationship allowed me to learn what truly mattered: what music I loved, how I preferred to spend my free time, even my favorite way to eat a steak.

Paul and I married in 2005 and started to grow our family the following year. During that time, I continued to realize success in my professional career and spent significant time serving my community. To everyone around me, I had it all: a handsome, loving husband, two beautiful daughters, and a successful career that continued to grow.

Although I was aware and grateful for a wonderful life, inside I still labeled myself as "divorced."

I'm sure it had something to do with my parents' relationship and their commitment to each other. They had married in 1970, and though there had been challenges and struggles, they managed to work through them and are still together today.

I, on the other hand, had achieved so much and was good at leading and making difficult decisions but had totally missed the mark in my previous relationship. I was having a hard time forgiving myself. So even though my new marriage was solid and built on mutual admiration and respect, I couldn't shake the "divorced" label.

Thirteen years into my marriage to the man I am meant to be with, I would still say, "I'm married, but he's my second husband..." I thought that I had healed all that was broken, but clearly I hadn't.

In 2018, I stumbled upon an opportunity called the 21-Day Unstoppable Influence challenge and the coaching of Natasha Hazlett. I had started to focus on personal growth and development as a way to gain some confidence. I was a budding entrepreneur and thought a stronger, more confident me would translate into a more successful business. And it has, but the internal work gave me so much more.

Later that year, I participated in another Unstoppable Influence challenge, where I opted to work with an accountability coach. On the intake form, I was asked to share a little bit about myself.

I typed in my usual spiel: "I'm married…he's my second husband…we have two kids. I work at a small, private liberal arts college…"

At our first meeting, my coach asked me a question that I couldn't answer.

"This is the second time you've introduced yourself to me and said that Paul isn't your first husband. But you met him more than 15 years ago. Why is that still part of your story?" Mic drop!

I thought hard, and there was a long awkward silence. I didn't really know. I couldn't answer her that night. So she challenged me to sit with that and unpack it.

I thought, *Why AM I holding onto that? Why IS that still part of my story?*

For days after, I couldn't stop thinking about it. I pondered, I journaled, and at some point, it finally came to me: I was ashamed and embarrassed that I had been divorced, that I had made such a poor life choice.

As I reflected on that and what it really meant, I realized that I wouldn't be the woman I am today without all of those experiences.

I'm strong, I'm confident, I use my voice, and I'm a leader. Until 2018, I saw my first marriage as something to be ashamed or embarrassed of, when really it has given me the strength to grow into the person I am today. My divorce isn't something to be ashamed of at all; it is something to embrace because look where I am now!

No longer shattered and broken, but **whole**.

I am so proud of the person I've become. The therapy years ago allowed me to process much of the baggage from that first relationship, which led me to choose a better partner the second time around.

The personal development work and introspection that has become such an integral part of my life since 2018 has opened my mind to new perspectives. I did a lot of that work on my own, but without the Unstoppable Influence community and partnering with a coach,

I would never have attained my empowering change in outlook.

Processing my feelings of shame around my divorce and feeling whole is a gift. I use that experience to find courage whenever I am fearful about making a change. I'm a happier person, and I no longer get derailed when I'm not someone's cup of tea. This peace with myself and my past allows me to dream crazy, big, audacious goals. It gives me the confidence to try new things and be comfortable in the event that they don't work out the way I had planned.

As a result of my internal work and beginning to feel whole, I had the confidence to put myself out there. I campaigned for a seat on my city's board of education and won. Two years later, I was elected as the chairperson. I've used my voice to speak in city council chambers, in press conferences on TV, and on stages at graduations.

Friend, if you are feeling less than whole, whether it be from a divorce or something else, I encourage you to gather up the strength and the confidence and do the internal work to process your feelings, so you can shed the labels that are limiting your potential.

You are *not* broken. You are perfectly imperfect, and you are a gift to the world.

KEY TAKEAWAYS

✦ When you are going through something hard, don't discount the power of therapy. It can be so helpful to talk to a professional who has helped others navigate similar struggles.

✦ It can be life-changing to find a community and connections where you can be vulnerable and feel supported and accepted as you are.

✦ Even if you have spent years thinking your divorce is an embarrassment or failure, it can actually be the event that sets you on a path to the person you were meant to be: peaceful, fulfilled, and whole.

FREE YOURSELF

1. Take some time to journal about what you truly think about your divorce or whatever is making you feel less than whole.

2. Once you identify some labels that have stuck over time, be patient with yourself, and understand that the process of letting go from your old label takes time.

3. Find a community of like-minded people who share your struggle, a therapist, or a coach who can help you "go deep" on the why behind the feelings.

CHAPTER 22

FROM TOO SENSITIVE TO GIFTED EMPATH

by Kristin Oakley

*If you feel like you don't fit into the world you
inherited, it is because you were born to help
create a new one.*

— Ross Caligiuri

"You're too sensitive."

"Why does that bother you so much? You shouldn't let
it."

"Why are you crying?"

"You need to develop a thicker skin."

"You have to toughen up!"

I can't recall the first time I heard these words; all I
know is that these were consistent messages I received
throughout my formative years. They usually came

from well-meaning authority figures in my life, including teachers, coaches, and family members.

Growing up, I also learned that tears were not welcome and should be stifled whenever possible...or I should at least wait until I was alone before allowing them to fall.

Apparently, I was too much for people in certain ways (too sensitive) and not enough in others (not tough enough).

I felt that something was wrong with me, that I must be defective. As a high-achieving people pleaser, I wanted to "fix" this perceived weakness in myself because I wanted to be strong!

So I did my best to stuff my feelings. In the movie *Frozen*, Queen Elsa captured my preferred coping strategy best when she said, "Conceal, don't feel."

Around the age of 12, I began experiencing a lot of digestive problems, which I am still healing from 30 years later. Looking back, I'm sure that all of my "stuffing" and attempts to suppress what I felt didn't help the situation.

This feeling of defectiveness followed me right into adulthood. A series of questions constantly went through my mind.

Why do I...

...sense and notice things that others do not?

...feel other people's emotions so deeply?

...feel so exhausted all the time, like I am fighting a constant battle against overwhelm?

Why does...

...being on social media absolutely drain and deplete me?

...being around infants or small children stress me out and produce feelings of fear, anxiety, and overwhelm instead of joy and excitement?

A consistent cry from my heart became...

What's wrong with me?

Why can't I just be normal?

Life would be SO much easier if I could just be like everyone else so I wouldn't notice so much or feel so overwhelmed.

I assumed that everyone else felt the absorbed emotions of others around them, the overwhelm caused by excessive stimulation, and the exhaustion that can come from sensory overload. I just thought that they could cope better, that they had learned to control, lessen, and suppress it all. I had no clue how others did it though. Was it even possible?

I concluded that to function in this world, I just needed to try harder and numb myself from the emotions, energies, and feelings while pretending that I didn't notice them.

In the spring of 2019, I hit a wall. By that time, I'd been working as a professional speaker for almost 18 years. During the previous five years, I'd traveled Monday through Saturday most weeks of the year, presenting anywhere from two to eight times a week to audiences of all sizes.

I continuously felt sick and tired. My general practitioner assured me that once my travel slowed down, I would feel better. Unfortunately, that wasn't the case. I finally went and saw a naturopathic doctor, who accurately diagnosed multiple issues negatively affecting my health.

"Clearly, you seem to handle all the stress and demands of your job quite well. But your lab results tell me that your body is *not*."

That was my first wake-up call. My second one came in the spring of 2021.

Having been laid off from my corporate speaking job during the height of COVID in 2020, I was working full-time as a personal empowerment and speaker coach. While I enjoyed serving the women I was working with, I felt *just* as exhausted as I had been while traveling.

I began questioning myself. *Why am I so tired all the time? Am I really cut out to be a coach? Do I have what it takes?*

During a session with my coach, Mandy, I expressed my frustrations.

She replied, "I have a book I want you to read. It's called *The Empath's Survival Guide* by Judith Orloff. I think it will really help you."

I had heard the term *empath* before and had thought it was a woo-woo, out-there concept. But I was open to Mandy's advice, so I ordered the book.

I felt led to get away and have what I call a "silent re-treat"—a few days away at a quiet location where I could be alone with the Lord to pray, read the book, journal, and process it all.

I booked an Airbnb by the ocean, and over three days, I read the book cover to cover. I hadn't even made it through the first chapter before tears started streaming down my cheeks.

It was as if the last 41 years of my life *finally* made sense. I realized that there wasn't anything *wrong* with me; there were actually a lot of things *right*!

I learned that there's a difference between having em-pathy, when your heart goes out to another person in joy or in pain, and being an empath, which means you actually *feel* others' emotions, energy, and physical symptoms in your own body without the usual defenses that most other people have.

I learned that there are different kinds of empaths, and to my surprise, I scored off the charts on each of the assessments provided. I learned that empaths have extremely reactive neurological systems and don't possess the same filters that other people have to block out stimulation. As a result, we absorb into our own bodies the feelings and energies of those around us.

I learned multiple strategies for developing healthy coping mechanisms to protect myself from overwhelm in this high-stimulus world, and that it was still possible for me to be myself and nurture my gifts of creativity, intuition, empathy, and spiritual connection. That it was possible to not just survive with these traits, but to thrive.

It turns out, my innate traits of high sensitivity are completely normal!

High sensitivity is a normal, biological individual difference in personality and physiology. One in five people are born as highly sensitive persons (HSPs); in other words, we make up about 20% of the population.

The problem is that most HSPs do not even know that they are one because this biological difference is not common knowledge.

Research shows that the brains of HSPs actually work a little differently, and it affects everything that we do. As a group, we are more reflective. We learn more slowly but thoroughly and tend to be unusually conscientious.

It also affects many of our bodily responses. For example, we tend to be more sensitive to things like…

- ✦ Caffeine
- ✦ Hunger
- ✦ Light
- ✦ Medications
- ✦ Pain
- ✦ Temperature

Because our brains process information and reflect on it more deeply, HSPs are more aware of subtleties. We notice things that others miss. This explains why I'm more easily overwhelmed: I feel and think about everything so much that I tend to be more overstimulated by what is going on around me.

Overall, I've learned that I need more downtime to compensate for my HSP traits.

In cultures where sensitivity is not valued, HSPs tend to be told things like, "Don't be so sensitive," which leads to them feeling abnormal and confirms their sense that there *is* something wrong with them.

Since we HSPs are a minority, if we're compared to the other 80% of the population, we can easily appear abnormal. However, that label is not true.

The truth is the reminder in God's word: "[He] created my inmost being; [He] knit me together in my mother's womb... I am fearfully and wonderfully made." (Psalm 139:13-14)

That includes all of my innate, highly sensitive traits! These HSP characteristics are all gifts from Him, *not* a curse. These qualities are the reasons I've been described as a sought-after coach, a heart-centered emcee, and an effective and powerful keynote speaker. I am a gifted empath—my sensitivity is a strength!

If you can relate to these characteristics check out some of the resources provided below. Know that you are not alone and you are not defective. There is nothing wrong with you! You have been wired this way on purpose, for a purpose. So embrace, celebrate, and encourage this strength and the unique gifts that your sensitivity and depth of feeling can provide to our hurting world.

KEY TAKEAWAYS

✦ If you have ever been shamed for your sensitivity or had it labeled as a "weakness," you are not alone.

✦ One in five people are born as highly sensitive persons (HSPs); we make up 20% of the population!

✦ HSP traits are normal and innate. The brains of HSPs work differently than the majority of the population, affecting everything that we do.

✦ Some HSP strengths include depth of processing, capacity for empathy, positive emotional responses, and sensing subtleties that others often miss.

✦ With these gifts also comes the challenge of being easily overstimulated and overwhelmed. Being aware of how highly stimulating situations affect HSPs, it may be helpful to prioritize more downtime so that they can process all they've taken in.

✦ Remember, there is nothing wrong with you. Your sensitivity is a strength and a gift! God created you this way for a reason, and our world desperately needs what you have to offer through your sensitivity.

FREE YOURSELF

1. If you suspect that you might be an HSP, check out these resources to learn more. Each of these books includes assessments that can help you determine whether you or someone you love are highly sensitive persons and/or empaths.

   - *The Empath's Survival Guide: Life Strategies for Sensitive People* by Judith Orloff, MD

   - *The Highly Sensitive Person: How to Thrive When the World Overwhelms You* by Elaine N. Aron, PhD

   - *Sensitive & Strong: A Guide for Highly Sensitive Persons and Those Who Love Them* by Denise J. Hughes and Cheri Gregory

2. If you are an HSP, spend time celebrating all the gifts God has equipped you with through your innate traits of sensitivity. Rather than seeing it as a weakness, reframe it as a strength and an opportunity for God to use you in unique ways.

3. If either you or someone you love is an HSP/empath, how are you navigating the challenges and rewards that come with these innate traits? How can this knowledge increase your understanding, grace, and compassion for yourself or for others who are wired differently from you?

CHAPTER 23

FROM WORTHLESS TO WORTHY

by Oneisis Frias

Just like moons and like suns, with the certainty of tides, just like hopes springing high, still I'll rise.

— "Still I Rise" by Maya Angelou

For years, I didn't know my worth. Every time someone good walked into my life, I determined they were "too good to be true" and assumed they would exit my life as quickly as they arrived once they got to know the real me and saw how worthless I was.

I felt like I didn't deserve good things in life, and if anything positive happened, I didn't trust it. I was always waiting for the other shoe to drop.

How did I get here? Growing up, I never had a lot of friends, because I always felt like they were too good for me. They had "normal" parents and healthy, loving families who enjoyed each other's company.

My parents divorced when I was two. My father was an alcoholic who popped in and out of my life. I didn't even see him from the age of 8 until I was 14 years old. My mother and stepfather chose drugs over my well-being my entire childhood, and my dad was never around.

By the tender age of 10, I was responsible for looking after my 8-year-old brother. I had to figure out how we would eat each day. Sometimes I would walk three miles with my brother to the mall, where we would get food samples for our dinner. Sometimes we would sneak into the movies after eating.

I always tried to make life a little more fun for my little brother, like those trips to the mall, so he wouldn't see the hell that we were living in at home.

When he asked me why things like our TV were disappearing from our house, I'd make up stories to protect him from our reality, which was that my stepfather was selling our belongings to purchase drugs.

I remember having to quickly clean up the burnt spoons my mom used to cook their drugs and learn how to mask their pungent smell in the hopes that my brother wouldn't notice and start asking me questions, the answers to which would rob him of his childlike innocence.

For years, I wondered...

Am I not worthy of them changing?

Am I not enough to make them see how much their actions are affecting me and my brother?

I never came up with a good answer.

Eventually, I grew numb to the pain of seeing my mother do drugs and live a promiscuous life. Her selfish choices were a hard pill to swallow at the time, but I couldn't do anything about it, so I chose to hide my feelings.

I was ashamed of her drug addiction and promiscuity. I was ashamed that every three months we'd have to move because their money was spent on drugs. I was especially ashamed that my mother used me and my brother to steal food to eat.

So I made it a personal mission to make myself invisible to avoid people asking questions that might make matters worse for me and my brother: them calling child protective services. My biggest fear was to be separated from my brother and be put into "the system."

As a child, I had no one to run to for help and no one to guide me. The very people who should have protected me were too caught up in their own lives. We had no relatives nearby to take care of us because my mother had pushed them all away.

In spite of all of that, at 10 years old, I somehow *knew* there was more to this chaos I was living in. There was something out there…something unexplainable that was fueling a desire within me. All I needed was time to ignite that fire within.

As Maya Angelou once said: "I can be changed by what happens to me. But I refuse to be reduced by it."

By the age of 12, things had gotten so bad at home that I made my first suicide attempt. I was willing to die just to ensure that I was noticed, that I mattered, and that I was loved.

I thought that through my nonexistence, my mother would see that what she was doing to me and my brother had caused so much pain that I no longer wanted to live. Maybe after my death she would at least choose to be there for my brother. Maybe he would have a better life because of my sacrifice.

It isn't easy or comfortable to write these words. My mother, may God rest her soul, was not a bad mother at all. She just made poor choices that affected my brother and me tremendously.

There were days when she was sober and was loving, attentive, and dedicated. Unfortunately, those days were few and far between.

Fortunately, that day, God had other plans for me and my life.

My 11-year-old brother found me unconscious on the bathroom floor. In his innocence, he just thought I had passed out from drinking because by that time, I had already experimented with alcohol to numb my pain.

When I woke up, I realized I had been lying there for hours. I could not believe that from the time I took the pills to the moment I awoke, no one had noticed. No one even knew I was gone!

I breathed deep, hugged my brother, and laughed it off. To keep him from worrying about me, I told him I had been too drunk to fall asleep on my bed.

Another time, I ran away from home for over 10 hours, but no one came looking for me.

I didn't see the point of living, and I didn't want to continue living with the amount of pain I was feeling at the time. So for a second time, I attempted suicide. This time, I made sure I was alone, hoping that the bottle of pills I swallowed that night would finally do the trick. To my surprise, I woke up later as if nothing had happened.

Years passed. Instead of further suicide attempts, I began to cut myself in places no one could see. It's not as if anyone would notice anyway, right?

At the same time, I played it smart and learned to hide everything very well. I got good grades in school and participated in events. I was smiling on the outside and dying on the inside, as I shoved my emotions deep within me. For me, cutting was a way of solidifying that I was still alive physically. This was also the point where my eating disorder began, stuffing my emotions with food, then throwing it back up to let the emotions out.

I became a pro at masking the pain and sadness I was feeling. Yet as much as I tried, there were still bursts of *Why am I even here?* playing in my mind.

At the beginning of my senior year in high school, I attempted suicide for a third time. *This time*, I thought, *if I add some liquor to the mix, it will work.*

It didn't.

I had tried to take my life three times and had failed every single time.

I FAILED!

I thought, *How worthless and unworthy am I that I could not even succeed at taking my own life?*

I prayed for God to show me my purpose in life because I was not seeing my own worth or how I could meaningfully contribute to the world.

Then I received news that rocked my world—I was pregnant!

I was 17 at the time. This pregnancy was my miracle from above. Knowing that I was about to become a mother helped me realize that I had more to live for. I now had a purpose: to be a mother!

My faith slowly began to grow stronger because I felt that there was finally someone looking out for me. Life handed me my angel in the time I needed it most.

Divine timing is what I call it. I don't believe in coincidences. I believe in God-incidences. He literally breathed a new life inside of me!

I thought this was my light at the end of a horrific tunnel, but the pain and heaviness did not stop just because I was expecting a child. Throughout my whole pregnancy, I was physically and mentally broken into a million pieces.

The one thing that kept me alive was the fact that I was carrying another human, and I knew I needed to stay alive for him. He provided me with an indescribable internal strength.

Then God, in His sovereign love for me, allowed me to meet a special person who showed me what true love was supposed to look like.

After years of searching for other people's recognition and love, I finally realized that the love I needed most was love from ME to me.

I needed to love myself. I didn't need to have others define my worth.

I am worthy. As a Believer, I have discovered how God sees me: WONDERFULLY MADE. I am God's masterpiece, worthy of all the greatest things that life has to offer!

Once I began to love myself and see my worth as a child of God, I began to finally live my life instead of just trying to survive. I finally began to experience true happiness.

My self-love and ability to experience true happiness allowed me to begin to truly love others as well.

I am now a wife of 25 years, a mother of two miracles, and a successful business owner.

As an adult, I was able to reconcile my tumultuous childhood with the following acknowledgement: My parents, may they both rest in peace, loved me the only way they knew how.

Today, I'm in charge of how I see myself. I live each day knowing that I'm here on purpose and for a purpose. My memories of the past will stay with me always. I am grateful to have learned from it all. I know now, more than ever, my purpose is to shine my light so brightly that it will illuminate the pathway for others to see their own way out.

Is the pain still there? Yes, it is. However, it no longer defines my worth. I am worthy.

KEY TAKEAWAYS

✦ You are here to be authentically YOU. The world needs your light.

✦ Remember that giving up would be robbing you of all you can do in your life. You and your story can be a light in the darkness for others.

✦ There is freedom in forgiveness. Holding on to resentment will only block you from being who you are meant to be authentically.

FREE YOURSELF

1. Make a list of where you want to be and how you want to feel. Find or create affirmations that will help you achieve those goals.

2. Use those affirmations to give yourself grace daily. When in doubt, pull out that list!

3. Take a few minutes each day to just BE. Close your eyes, relax, and breathe. Inhale for eight counts, hold for eight counts, and exhale for eight counts...until you feel calm and centered.

CHAPTER 24

FROM ABANDONED TO RESTORED

by Marilyn Hart

*If you're getting abandonment, if you're getting
abuse as a child, if you're getting uncertainty
when you're a child, unfortunately you tend to
look for that in your life later on and you think
that's love.*

— Sebastian Stan

I remember it like it was yesterday. Me as a five-year-old girl on my first flight ever, from Oregon to Hawaii. It was a long flight, and my ears were hurting to the point of tears. The flight attendants tried to help, but my parents didn't know what to do, so they just told me to be a good girl and be quiet. I obliged through the pain.

On that vacation in paradise, I went to the most amazing luau with my parents. It was magical seeing the hula girls dance with beautiful flowers in their hair while I watched the men dance the ring of fire.

The next day, my family went shopping at a big souvenir store. I got lost in the hula section trying to recreate what I had seen the night before. Suddenly, a security guard walked up and asked me where my parents were because the store was now closed and locked.

I had no idea they were gone!

I started crying. I felt like I had been abandoned by my parents in a store in an unfamiliar place. After what seemed like eternity, we were reunited.

When I look back at my life, these are just a couple of the many examples where I was left alone and did not have my needs met. I just wanted love and attention. I got neither from my parents.

This desire for love and attention led me to meeting my future husband at the tender age of 15. He showered me with love, attention, and affection. I spent so much time with him that I ended up pulling away from my friends.

Little did I know, I was being groomed by a narcissist. We married when I was 21. I started to see signs of his narcissism early, but I didn't know any better. As far as I was concerned, I had signed up for better or worse, so I was going to stick it out.

Three months after moving our entire family across the country, he told me that he wanted a divorce. He was spending a lot of time with my girlfriend, and I suspected that they were having an affair of the heart. He denied it of course, but I trusted my intuition.

After 21 years of marriage and 27 years together, I found myself in a role I had never imagined: a single mom of four children (ages 4, 6, 12, and 14).

I tried desperately to do all the "right" things: therapy, being there for my kids, smiling, and being happy. I went through the motions, but I was stuck in what I call the "messy middle" for far too long.

I felt like I was on the hamster wheel of life, running from one thing to the next and never dealing with the pain from my marriage or my childhood.

Shortly after my divorce was finalized, I entered into another unhealthy relationship, this time with an alcoholic. I recognized the signs early but didn't think I was worthy of anything better. He treated me well, but I was lonely because alcohol was his first love.

I finally summoned up the strength and left him so I could work on myself.

Unfortunately, I ended up in a tailspin of self-destructive behavior because I still didn't believe I was worthy of love. Due to my need to be loved, I lacked self-control and put myself in risky situations with alcohol and men.

I thought maybe someone would love me if I was thinner, good at sex, or under the influence of alcohol. So I went on extreme diets, woke up in unfamiliar places, and risked my life for love and attention.

Why was I doing this to myself?

After over four years of debauchery, I met someone who I thought was the love of my life. He had addiction issues and did not manage his finances well, and I saw the signs right in front of me, but as usual, I ignored them. I was willing to accept the circumstances because I didn't want to be alone.

Nothing got better. Then COVID hit, and my loneliness became nearly insurmountable.

During this time, I started doing some inner work to examine myself.

Why wasn't I worthy of love?

Why didn't I like being alone?

One day while in an intensive personal empowerment coaching program, I was watching a video by Dr. Gabor Maté. He talked about the basic human needs of attachment and authenticity. This really resonated with me, and I finally understood what I had been missing. I was not being true to myself (lack of authenticity), and my needs weren't being met (lack of attachment).

I started to cry. I knew in that moment that I needed to break up with my boyfriend.

I had a coaching session with another participant in the program, and she sensed an energy shift when I talked about him. It was a powerful confirmation that I was on the right track.

Although I was initially afraid that I was going to lose connections with all my new friends and his family when we broke up, I discovered that those people loved me for who I am, and we still remain good friends.

It took a lot of strength and courage to break up with my boyfriend, but my Unstoppable Influence tribe gave me so much love, support, and encouragement. It was exactly what I needed in order to continue my healing journey.

Sometimes moving forward past our greatest fears provide the greatest breakthroughs!

With that toxic relationship behind me, I began to dig deeper and evaluated all my past relationships. I discovered that there were many similarities.

I was repeatedly sacrificing my own needs so I wouldn't be alone.

As I journeyed even deeper, I realized that I had abandonment issues from my childhood.

To the outside world, I had a seemingly great life. My parents owned a business and worked really hard. I had everything I wanted...except for the two things that mattered most to me: their time and attention.

I spent a lot of time home alone as I was growing up. As a result, I craved attention—from anyone, even people who weren't good for me.

I also realized that I was starting to repeat some unhealthy patterns from my wild-child days in my dating life. I knew intellectually that I was worthy of love, but I still wasn't there emotionally.

Now that I understand narcissism, my abandonment issues, and my feelings of unworthiness when it comes to love, I have been able to start doing the real work to move forward.

I decided that I have to change my patterns and beliefs about love in order to truly be happy and get what I want in life. Yet I had no idea what I needed to do in order to make this change.

Fortunately, in July 2019, I found the Unstoppable Influence community through a 21-Day Challenge. I started to remove my "bricks" about narcissism and relationships. After the challenge, I felt a little bit better and decided to sign up for the annual Unstoppable

Influence Summit in October. What an amazing three-day, life-changing experience!

I had never heard such uplifting content and been around so many positive women. I felt that I was divinely called to be a part of the community, so I joined the Unstoppable Influence Inner Circle. What a gift and blessing to myself! I dove in and participated in all the training.

I learned to use meditation and make shifts in my mindset, down to even the simplest of everyday words.

I continued to delve deeper into my behaviors as I became a Certified Personal Empowerment Coach. I gained a lot of insight into how to ask powerful questions to think through situations and gain clarity.

I used cord-cutting exercises to visualize myself breaking the "cord" from people or thoughts that no longer served me.

I discovered that abundance is my birthright and that I can manifest anything I want—it just takes work and focus to shift my thoughts.

I am a different person today than I was two years ago, but I'm still on my healing journey—because it's truly a journey, not a destination.

I went from feeling abandoned to feeling restored. Change is happening rapidly for me. It only took one decision and one step to start moving forward.

While this has been challenging and hard work, I surrounded myself with positive people who encouraged me to keep going.

One day at a time, I'm taking care of myself and no longer just existing. Now I'm really smiling, and I feel like I've abandoned the old me and am restored to the new me. The best is yet to come!

KEY TAKEAWAYS

✦ Take the first step and make a decision to do the work, then take one more step and then another and another.

✦ Don't stop doing the work, even though it's hard. You might have to make some tough choices, but keep going because it's worth it.

✦ You may have setbacks, but don't let that stop you from moving forward.

✦ Celebrate your successes, however small or big. Don't beat yourself up for the past. You are moving forward!

✦ Most importantly, be grateful for your journey. You wouldn't be the incredible woman you are today without your unique experiences.

FREE YOURSELF

1. Every day before you get out of bed, write or recite at least three things you're grateful for. This helps to shift your vibration and can even have a positive effect on those around you.

2. Listen to a meditation while falling asleep at night. Your brain will soak up all the positive information, even when you're asleep!

3. Look in the mirror and tell yourself "I love you!" Start saying positive words to yourself about how amazing you are. You will start to feel a difference in your mood and attitude.

4. Most importantly, smile and try to have fun! LIVE again instead of just existing.

CHAPTER 25

FROM PROBLEM TO WONDERFULLY MADE

by Vanessa Bryson

For you formed my inward parts; you knitted me together in my mother's womb. I praise you, for I am fearfully and wonderfully made.

— Psalm 139:13-14 (ESV)

I heard the familiar little poem so many times throughout my life. "Sticks and stones may break my bones, but words will never hurt me."

And I want to call BS on that.

If you get a broken bone from a stick or a stone, chances are you're not going to remember it for long. You won't recall how it happened, nor will the pain last for years.

But when people say certain things to you, you just can't unhear them. You can't forget.

I have had many significant people in my life tell me that I was the problem. When those negative words come from people of authority—those who we believe are here to love us, nurture us, and encourage us—it's easy to believe what they say.

Even years after the words were uttered, I would get into a negative headspace and start beating myself up, allowing them to flood my mind and hurt me, and I'd start believing them all over again.

However, holding on to negative thoughts and the negative opinions of other people harbors disease in our bodies and creates undue stress. It also can cause chemical reactions in our brain and body that can harm our health.

I know what I'm talking about firsthand because I am an ovarian cancer survivor.

Genetic testing has shown that my cancer was caused by the environment, so that means a chemical, something toxic. There are numerous things that contribute to environmental causes, and your surroundings and the ideas that you are feeding into your mind are all part of those contributions.

When I was first told that I had ovarian cancer, the very first thought that came to my mind was *I will not die from this*. I clung to that like a lifeline. I honestly believe that's why I have walked this path with as much ease and less hardship than others have.

However, in the beginning I had a lot of soul-searching to do. I had to dig deep within myself to find the answers. I had to talk myself off the proverbial ledge that I felt others had put me on when they were being ugly, mean, and disrespectful to me.

It wasn't just them, though. I realized that I also said things to myself that I would never dream of speaking to another human being. I spoke to and about myself with crushing words that hurt me to the core.

So if toxic words had possibly contributed to my ovarian cancer, in my journey to a restored health, I needed to find a way to stop speaking unkindly to myself and learn how to process those toxic words from other people.

On my quest to find answers, I immersed myself in self-help: motivational books and my Bible. There are many truths in the Bible, and there is a verse for almost anything that you're going through in life.

If you need help, pray to God and ask for help. You are never going to face things alone.

I went to God with my problem (toxic words), and He blessed me with an answer. Through His words in the Bible, I realized that the unkind words of other people—and the unkind words I spoke to myself—were all lies. I realized that I'm not a problem, as others had told me.

Neither are you. God created each of us with purpose and for a reason, for a time such as this.

If you're a strong, independent person, it is sometimes hard to ask for help. We like to feel that we can do things on our own and we can make our own way in life. And that's true—we can.

But wouldn't you rather have the love, guidance, and direction from your heavenly Father who loves you just the way you are, just the way He created you to be?

He knows the road that lies before you, so wouldn't you rather let Him direct your path than the negative words of people who are hurting as well and are just deflecting their hurt and anguish onto you?

In my five-year journey to fight cancer, some days were extremely hard. And on those hard days, my negative self-talk and the comments of others resurfaced. But then I remember that the Bible tells me I'm fearfully and wonderfully made. God knows the plans He has for me, and they are to prosper me, not harm me, and keep me free from disease. And I must rely on that.

Some days, I must recite that over and over in my mind. When I do, I'm building my synapses and neurons and all that neurological activity in my brain, making it stronger. The more times you practice things, the more easily it becomes routine. So the more times I practice telling myself that I'm here for a time such as this and that I'm fearfully and wonderfully made, I am building up a shield that protects me, and it helps. It protects me from those daggers and arrows, broken words, and hurt that people throw at me so that they don't stick to me. Instead, they bounce off me. That is my armor of protection.

I pray over myself every morning and ask that God be with me, that He will help me through the day, that He will guide and direct my steps, and that He will put people in my path who need to know who He is. Also, that I will recognize them, and that I will be able to speak Truth to them to help ease their burden and help lighten their loads.

None of us were put here on Earth to be junk. That is not part of the plan. God is loving, and you are wonderfully and reverently made.

I have approached healing my body from cancer in the same way as extracting other negativity such as hate and hurt and the toxicity from relationships that I have experienced in my life.

It's excavating your whole soul to just clear everything out.

To do that, it's time to get down to the core of who you truly are and start unpacking every lie that you've ever told yourself. Start Unbecoming who the world told you that you were. Because you are a child of God, the king of all kings, and He did not make you to be anything other than precious, loved, cared for, happy, healthy, and to have a service-minded heart.

He only wants the best for you. So why wouldn't you want the best for yourself?

As you walk this path, I encourage you to stay strong, stay focused, and keep looking up. Know that you're fearfully and wonderfully made and never fighting the fight alone.

KEY TAKEAWAYS

✦ The things that others say to you and about you are often lies that they are just projecting onto you. You do not need to take them on as truth.

✦ Holding on to negative thoughts and opinions of other people harbors disease in your body and creates undue stress that can harm your health.

✦ The Bible and self-help books can help you shift and strengthen your mindset.

FREE YOURSELF

1. Take a piece of paper, and fold it in half vertically so there's a left side and a right side. On the left, write down any negative thoughts you have. On the right, write down where you heard it. Is it something you told yourself, that someone else told you, or that you just picked up and started believing?

2. On a new sheet of paper, rewrite the negative though into positive form. Or if it is a bold-faced lie, say out loud, "This is a lie!" Then write the truth.

3. If anything about your true self comes to light that you do not like, work on those things. Pray to God to change how you feel about the situation, or ask Him for forgiveness so you can let go.

CHAPTER 26

FROM UNLOVED TO LOVED

by Tricia Speas

Whenever you feel unloved, unimportant, or insecure, remember to whom you belong.

— Ephesians 2:19-22

To feel loved is something I've wanted for as long as I can remember. Even though I believed my parents loved me, I often felt alone and unloved.

Growing up, the stigma of being a preacher's daughter hung over me and added to my feeling unloved, especially when I realized boys were too scared to pursue "the preacher's daughter."

In order to feel loved, I began turning to food. It was the best friend who was always there for me and the one who never ignored me. I could always count on food to make me feel better, if only for a short time.

In college, I met and married my husband, and I expected to be taken care of and to feel loved. Instead, my husband was so distant and laid-back that I found myself tackling responsibilities I believed were his job as the leader of our family.

I paid the bills, I served as the spiritual leader, and I made most decisions, all while doing my best to be submissive to him and support his dreams. But secretly, I felt very alone and unloved in our relationship, and I hated it, so I again soothed myself with the one thing that never failed to make me feel loved: food.

My husband and I both wanted kids, and the birth of our son, Gabe, was a joyful time. However, my husband was gone a lot coaching basketball, and I felt like I was raising our son on my own.

I became pregnant a second time, but it ended in a miscarriage. Four months into my third pregnancy, the doctor could hear our baby's heartbeat. But at five months, the doctor pronounced our baby lifeless.

My fourth pregnancy also ended in miscarriage, and that's when I decided I would stop trying to have more children. My husband, perhaps devastated by his own grief, was no comfort through any of these miscarriages. So not only did I feel more alone and unloved than you can imagine, I also felt sure there must be something wrong with me.

Why couldn't I carry a baby to term? Was I not good enough to have more children? Was I an awful parent? I even questioned God for letting this happen and briefly wondered if He, too, had abandoned me.

Through all this I continued to pack on the pounds, only to put myself through more diets…and more failure. I became a secret eater to hide my shame at failing to lose the weight, yet I absolutely loved food because it was always there for me, even when others weren't.

I was 38 when I started feeling very sick. A visit to the doctor revealed that I was pregnant again. Terrified that this baby wouldn't make it either, I kept my pregnancy secret for a long time.

At seven months pregnant, I agreed to help care for my sick parents so my brother and his wife—their usual caretakers—could attend a conference. My mom struggled with severe dementia, and my father was dying of bone cancer.

While visiting with my parents on their patio, my water broke. In a panic, I grabbed Gabe and headed to a hospital I did not know, in an unfamiliar city. After lying in that strange hospital for a week, with only my twelve-year-old son by my side, I was transported back to Tulsa and immediately diagnosed with Group B/ Beta Strep. Doctors performed a C-section in order to save both my life and my baby's.

I will never forget them rolling my bed into the Intensive Baby Care Unit to see my precious four-pound son, who I named Nate.

During this time, my husband and I were operating our own lawn maintenance and landscaping business, which was quite lucrative. But he decided to sell it and chase some other dream he thought would make us quicker money.

I did my best to support him, but things got so bad that we were in danger of losing our house. I couldn't stand by and allow that to happen, so I took on two, sometimes three, jobs at a time to help our family make ends meet. I did this all while raising our boys alone because my husband was always working.

By the time Gabe went to college, I was hanging on by a thread. Food was the only companion I had...the only thing that seemed to fill that need I had to feel loved and valued.

My mother eventually passed away, and on that same day, I discovered my husband was having an affair. I was so angry I couldn't properly grieve her. I've never felt more unloved.

After my husband and I split, I still longed for companionship, so I put myself out there. On two different occasions, men told me I was not a match for them because I was too fat.

Eventually I remarried, but the marriage only lasted a year. It started out wonderfully, but then the verbal abuse began. I remember my second husband once telling me to "get my fat ass in the house where it belonged." Once again, I was reminded of how unloved I was.

Life as a single mom was hard. I worked a lot, sacrificing time with my boys just to pay the bills and put food on the table. All the while turning to my ever-present friend, food, to keep me going.

After my boys grew up and left home, the wife of a former third-grade student of mine reached out to me. She wanted to meet. I agreed. We enjoyed a long talk, and then she introduced me to a group of women.

Meeting them changed my life, and things finally began to turn around for me.

This group of wonderful women truly loved and encouraged me. They shared tools I could use to help me through situations where I felt alone and unloved. And when my passion for caregiving came to light, I became a certified nursing assistant and began a new journey… one I might never have discovered had I not said yes to their friendship and support.

These women helped me see that I am not "an obese woman with no value," as I once thought. Instead, I am an amazing, courageous, smart, and successful woman who is full of love, compassion, and encouragement.

Best of all, they helped me see that I am loved, and that while I often felt alone, I never was. My God was always with me, even when I didn't realize it. I started leaning more into Him, too, because I know His love is perfect. He loves me regardless of my weight, my mistakes, and my struggles, and He encourages me to be all I can be.

My life now is good. I love who I am and am blessed with friends who love me for ME, not for who they think I "should" be.

No matter how unloved and unworthy you may feel right now, please remember that like me, you are loved. Your Heavenly Father loves you, and so will the right people for you. Find your people and let them—and God—love you until you learn to love yourself.

KEY TAKEAWAYS

✦ Even with the best of intentions, the people we grow up around and go into relationships with are not always capable of giving us the love we need.

✦ Food and other escapes may seem like a source of love, but they provide only the illusion of love.

✦ If you're in pain because you believe you're unloved and not valued, know that you are not alone in how you feel. Also know that your Heavenly Father loves you right where you are, and so will the right people for you.

FREE YOURSELF

1. Find and connect with positive people who are similar to you in faith, beliefs, struggles, and goals. If someone reaches out to you, agree to meet up with them and see how it goes. Just one person can make all the difference!

2. Make a list of things you like about yourself and that you do well. If you can't think of anything, write down the positive things others say about you. Keep your list with you and read it every time you feel unloved or unworthy.

3. Invite God to show you how much He loves you because He is with you, and He loves you more than you can imagine!

CHAPTER 27

NOW, IT'S YOUR TURN

"And you will know the truth, and the truth will set you free."

— John 8:32 (ESV)

You made it all the way to the end—congratulations! I pray that our stories have stirred your soul, and that your eyes have been opened to the lies spoken to you and about you for years.

Freedom begins with an awareness of the Truth.

Awareness, though, is just the first step.

Next, you need to make a decision.

The word decision comes from the Latin word *decidere*, which means to literally "cut off." As I teach in my first book, *Unstoppable Influence*, there is power when you truly make a "decision" as opposed to just a "choice." When you commit to consciously cut off other options.

Inky Johnson once said that, "Commitment is staying true to what you said you would do, long after the mood you said it in has left you."

There's immense power in a true decision. When each of us *decided* to renounce and reject the lies that we believed about ourselves, we were freed.

I want to invite you now to take out a piece of paper and begin to jot down all the lies and limited beliefs that you resonated with in this book. This is the perfect place to start.

If you are a Christian, invite the Holy Spirit into this time of reflection, and ask that He illuminate any of the lies that you've been believing and to reveal the Truth. Remember—when you ask, you receive, and when you seek, you will find. Jesus said in John 10:10 that the thief comes only to steal and kill and destroy, but He came so that we may have life and have it abundantly.

God wants you to know the Truth about who you are and how He made you. In fact, the Bible is filled with Truth about your identity in Christ.

To further support you, in the companion workbook, I have included a list of Truth and identity statements for God's children found in the Bible. You can download it for free at DesignYourBestLife.com/gift.

Next, break any agreements that no longer serve you using the three-step process outlined in Chapter 2:

1. Identify the agreement.

2. Renounce it.

3. Replace the lie with the Truth.

For stubborn, long-held limiting beliefs, consider working with a certified NLP practitioner or hypnotherapist. You can get access to a directory of them in the companion workbook.

To learn more about the Unstoppable Influence programs and how we can support you in the Unbecoming process and beyond, go to UnstoppableInfluence.com/programs.

One final tool that's been in my toolbelt for years and helped me recognize and free myself from lies I'd been believing is being in community with encouragers. The prefix *en* means "to put into," so an encourager is one who "puts you into courage."

An encourager is one who will speak truth to you, instead of just telling you what you want to hear. They will sharpen you and help you to be the very best version of yourself. They will lift you up and be the wind beneath your wings on the hard days. They will celebrate you and always build you up.

If you don't have a group of encouragers and would like to belong to our very special community, go to DesignYourBestLife.com/group and join us! We would be honored to support you.

Remember, this is a process, so give yourself grace. Each time a new lie pops up, practice breaking the agreement and replacing it with the Truth. The more you practice, the easier and more automatic it becomes.

You *can* take your life back from the one who seeks to sideline you from finding and fulfilling your purpose. I believe in you.

I cannot wait to hear your breakthrough to freedom story! Email me at hello@OurGatheringTable.com, and let me know how this book has changed your life.

NATASHA HAZLETT

Natasha Nassar Hazlett is an inspirational speaker, author, online business strategist, and attorney. She empowers women with the clarity, confidence, and strategies they need to boost their income and influence in the marketplace.

In addition to being a mentor and coach, she is the co-founder of Fast Forward Marketing, LLC and Our Gathering Table with her husband, Richard. Most importantly, though, she's mom to a precious girl and twin boys who are the light of her life.

The Hazletts have been honored twice with the prestigious ClickFunnels Two Comma Club award. The *Idaho Business Review* honored Natasha with their 2013 Idaho Women of the Year award, and she has been honored multiple times with the Rising Star Award by *Super Lawyers* magazine.

You can learn more about Natasha at: NatashaHazlett. com and her personal blog at: Faithfull.blog.

Join Natasha's community for women, Our Gathering Table, the place where women become friends at: OurGatheringTable.com.

Connect with Natasha:

Facebook: NatashaHazlett.com/FB

Instagram: NatashaHazlett.com/IG

YouTube: NatashaHazlett.com/YT

Podcast: DesignYourBestLife.com/Podcast

MARTHA BROGNARD

Martha L. Brognard is a Certified Personal Empowerment Coach and founder of Second Act Coaching With Martha. She believes your "Second Act" can be your best act!

As a highly trained coach, Martha sees where you are and where you want to be and helps you recognize what needs to shift to get you there. Together, you create a step-by-step plan to give you the clarity and confidence to live your Second Act (retirement and beyond) with joy and purpose.

Martha is spiritually grounded, practical, and resilient, but she also has a fun and adventurous side. She loves to take her clients on a fun-filled adventure so they create a purpose-driven and fulfilling Second Act they look at with pride, knowing they have made a difference.

After 31 years serving her country, Martha has chosen to serve more as a coach. She also has bachelor's and master's degrees in professional writing.

LISA CAIN

Lisa is blissfully married to her soulmate (a retired warden), mom to adult children and fur babies, and lover of all things sparkly! Her big personality, booming laugh, and enveloping hugs are accentuated by her tall stature. She can't easily be missed in a crowd!

Lisa's passion is coaching women and teens in understanding their unconscious limitations and creating strategies to overcome them. She regularly encourages the celebrations of daily wins resulting in her kids renaming Wednesdays as "Wins-days"! She hopes you'll implement this celebration practice with your family, friends, and coworkers. Let's normalize celebrating others as well as ourselves!

Lisa has found freedom in embracing her authentic self. She provides a daily "Tiaras aren't just for Tuesdays" message where she shares her personal struggles and daily aha's and encourages others to find their own personal sparkle even on the gloomiest of days. "Remember who you are, and straighten that tiara!"

DONNA CONNOR

Donna Connor is a proud wife and mom, serial entre-preneur, CEO of a multi-seven-figure consulting firm, NuQuo Group, and the founder of Life on Purpose Academy, where she helps people heal their relation-ship with money and live a life of purpose.

After growing up where there was never enough, she developed an unhealthy relationship with money that led to two bankruptcies before the age of 40. Since then, she has been able to recover from bankruptcy in record time, set herself and her husband up for retirement, be-come a financial advisor, start three highly successful businesses, and create a money legacy for her family.

ANDREA DELL

Andrea Dell supports high-octane, mission-driven women in sharing their message via relationship-building, income-producing written content.

In addition to writing copy and offering content training and coaching, Andrea is the author of the book *Dream Client Gold Mine* and a Certified Master Practitioner of NLP, hypnosis, and Time Line Therapy™.

Her personal mission is to facilitate hope and healing in the world.

GINA FAUST

Gina is a Certified Personal Empowerment Coach who helps women navigate relationships by developing communication and connectedness and setting measurable and attainable goals. She guides her clients to better understand themselves.

Gina's own life's journey has filled her cup with experiences that empower her to provide genuine, empathetic support to her clients.

Gina also enjoys helping her clients connect with their inner spiritual life, something that her degree in theology and time as a spiritual companion on retreats have uniquely equipped her to do.

As a Certified Master Practitioner and Coach of NLP, Time Line Therapy™, and hypnosis, Gina helps clients uncover limitations by breaking down mental barriers with the power of language, changing the way clients perceive the world in order to live the life they are dreaming of.

Gina believes every woman is honorable, beautiful, and courageous! She loves walking alongside her clients and celebrates every step along the way.

ONEISIS FRIAS

Oneisis Frias, founder of Faith Driven Soul, helps women learn how to navigate the storms in life and teaches self-love strategies to help them fulfill their purpose.

Oni, as she prefers to be called, believes in turning challenges in life into fuel to help pave the way for others. She has touched countless lives with her story and has learned how to take the bricks that life has thrown at her and use them to build her own castle.

She is a wife of 24 years, mother of two young men, and a commercial insurance business owner, and is pursuing her Bachelor of Science in Psychology.

Oni enjoys watching the sunrise at the beach. She has a deep connection with nature and uses this space to reflect, be grateful, and acknowledge her growth.

A woman of faith, Oni shares that clinging to the Lord during her toughest moments is what has kept her here on Earth.

ERIN GARDINER

Erin Gardiner lives in Saskatchewan, Canada, with her husband, two kids, and many pets.

She has a passion for helping others and is active in her community by coaching and serving on community boards.

When she's not acting as chauffeur to her kids, she enjoys reading, bowling, gardening, traveling, and camping with her family.

MARILYN J. HART

Marilyn Hart is a Certified Personal Empowerment Coach who specializes in helping women move through the messy middle of life after major transitions such as divorce, retirement, or moving, and even past family or relationship trauma.

As a single mom of four grown children, she retired from a 33-year career with the federal government and is embarking on her next adventures as a business management analyst and life transition coach helping women to grow and shine their light bright once again!

CHRISTINE HOY

Christine Hoy is an author, speaker, and follower of Jesus. A former women's Bible study leader, freelance writer, and life coach, in 2018, Christine took on the role of caregiver for her terminally ill mother. Three years later, she found herself physically exhausted, emotionally depleted, and completely burned out.

God invited Christine on a yearlong sojourn into a season of rest. Although initially resistant, she eventually surrendered her need to be in control and gave her plans and expectations to God. In doing so, Christine experienced healing, restoration, and unshakable peace unlike anything she had felt before. She shares what she learned in her upcoming book, *Peace Beyond Perfection: Overcoming The Fear Of Not Being Enough.*

In addition to writing, Christine is embracing her newest role as "Gigi" to her first grandchild. She and her husband live in Southport, North Carolina, with their white lab, Zeus.

KAREN KAHN

Karen Kahn is a Certified Emotion Code Practitioner who lives in Twin Falls, Idaho. She is an ordained minister with over 30 years of experience.

Karen is also an Unstoppable Influence Personal Empowerment Coach and a Certified Master Practioner and Coach of NLP, Time Line Therapy™ and Hypnosis..

Karen has a passion for helping others release the negative energies and emotional blocks keeping them from stepping out and becoming all they were created to be.

When she is not working, Karen enjoys hiking, biking, kayaking, snowshoeing, or just spending time with friends enjoying the great Idaho outdoors.

CASSANDRA LENNOX

Cassandra aims to inspire and make a lasting impact on others' lives with her words. She is the author of five books, including reimagined nursery rhymes and inspirational books for teens and adults.

Through freelancing and ghostwriting, she has personally helped hundreds of individuals get their words out to the world so they can make the impact they were meant to and shine their light while unleashing their truth and gifts.

A firm believer that we should not only Dream Big, but also consistently pursue our dreams, Cassandra is a lifelong student and advocate in the personal growth and development space and always open to opportunities to assist and encourage others to thrive.

When she isn't writing, this mom of four loves quality time with her children and welcomes new adventures with open arms. She enjoys travel, cooking, trivia and board games, connecting with friends, laughter, and embracing the journey.

MISTY K. LYON

Misty Lyon is on a mission to help individuals and teams identify "The Next Best Step," so they can build rapid momentum toward achieving their goals. She helps her clients uncover blocks that have held them back from reaching their objectives, then empowers them to sift through multiple opportunities to determine which ones will bear the best fruit, so they can keep more of their two most precious commodities—their time and resources.

Misty is a Certified Personal Empowerment Coach and Certified Master NLP, Time Line Therapy™, and hypnosis practitioner.

When Misty is not speaking onstage or working with clients, she is enjoying time with her son and their dog. She's a self-proclaimed personal development junkie who enjoys horseback riding with her besties and downtime, including enjoying the hot tub.

KRISTIN OAKLEY

Kristin Oakley is a professional keynote speaker, emcee, National TV Host, and Certified Personal Empowerment Coach, with over 20 years of public speaking and presenting experience across multiple industries. She has traveled throughout North America as a presenter for several Fortune 500 brands—and was even a guest presenter on QVC!

Named the 2020 Unstoppable Influencer of the Year, Kristin is a professional member of the National Speakers Association, the creator of The Unstoppable Speaker Program, The Unstoppable Speaker Coach, a licensed WomanSpeak Circle Leader, and a certified WomanSpeak Coach. She is also the founder of Speak and Shine, which helps women own their brilliance through the art of speaking.

She loves spending time at her home in North Carolina with her husband, Charlie, and their two entertaining cats, Cosmo and Zander. Her favorite hobbies include horseback riding and singing her heart out at Keith Urban concerts.

COLLEEN REKERS

Colleen Rekers is an innovative transformational leadership coach, dynamic speaker, international best-selling author, and serial entrepreneur who is living the laptop lifestyle and running multiple lucrative businesses. She is a certified life and wellness coach, an Integrative Health Practitioner, and an expert in multiple holistic healing modalities. Her training, education, research, and life experience have catapulted her into the life, wellness, mindset, and personal development areas. With her unshakable belief and dedication to her clients, their success is inevitable.

Colleen Rekers resides in Northern California with her family of nine and passionately serves clients all around the world. She is known as a Supermom for her ability to empower women to obtain a higher degree of personal, professional, and financial freedom, allowing them to get clarity, release limiting beliefs, overcome overwhelm, find joy, and show up confident and stronger than ever for themselves and their families.

To learn more, go to ColleenRekers.com.

To apply to work with Colleen or her team, email colleen@colleenrekers.com.

Follow her on Instagram @colleenrekers, and subscribe to her YouTube channel at @colleenrekers3905.

MARIA DELORENZIS REYES

Maria DeLorenzis Reyes is a Jersey girl through and through. Born and bred in the Garden State, Maria spends her life fighting for what's right—even if it means leaving her comfort zone. After years in the corporate world in New York City, Maria decided to follow her dreams and founded Training Innovations and MDR Brands in 2007.

As a mom to Christian, Maria is dedicated to helping others find their path to success through motivation and real talk. She is passionate about shining a light on the perspectives that aren't heard and pushing people to challenge their thinking and widen their view. On her *Finding The Upside* podcast, she interviews business leaders and everyday people, focusing on how to find opportunity in any challenge.

Maria enjoys cooking, traveling, and exploring new cultures and cuisines. She's an adventurer at heart, always looking for her next big challenge.

HEATHER ROMANSKI

Heather Romanski went to college to learn how to "work with computers," but quickly realized that she enjoyed working with people as much as machines. She graduated with a degree in Computer Science and Business Economics and then went on to earn her MBA.

Heather is the Director of Computer Support Services at Connecticut College, a private liberal arts college. Her position allows her to help faculty, staff, and students solve their technology issues with the perfect combination of skill and humor. In 2019, she was the winner of the college's Presidential Staff Award for Inspiration.

In 2018, Heather started her journey of personal development and now coaches women in the areas of leadership, growth mindset, self-advocacy, and boundary-setting.

She married Paul in 2005, and they are now raising two teenage daughters in southeastern Connecticut. They enjoy bowling, eating out, gathering with friends, and traveling, especially to the beach.

MAY SIMPSON

May Simpson is from Union City, Tennessee. She is a Certified Personal Empowerment Coach, with a focus on blended families. She helps them achieve a loving, harmonious environment so each family member feels loved, respected, and free to be themselves.

May knows the challenges that come from a blended family. At the age of 30, she found herself divorced with two small children, ages three and six months. She later remarried and her second husband, Joe, had two children, twins aged 11 at the time. They later adopted two more boys, making a beautiful yet complex family. They just celebrated their thirty-first anniversary.

Through her personal experience and professional training, she has a wealth of tools and knowledge to share with other families, including her book, *Life in the Blender: A Guide to Creating Harmony as a Blended Family.*

RUTH "ROOTY" SMITH

"Rooty" combines experience and training to provide faith-based coaching, helping individuals find and share their true selves. Her coaching draws from her 40+ years of public service supporting college students, concert and theater devotees, communities, families, contractors, and teammates. In each role, she helps participants find insights and move toward beneficial outcomes.

Ruth has an ever-growing relationship with the Lord. She and her husband recently celebrated their twentieth anniversary. They blended their families, sharing three dynamic children, who later added their sweet spouses and four wonderful grandchildren.

She is a certified Level Two Personal Empowerment Coach, NLP and hypnotherapy practitioner, author, contracting officer (CPPO/CPPB), musician, and speaker.

Rooty contributed to May Simpson's book *Life in the Blender: A Guide to Creating Harmony in a Blended Family*. Her own manuscript, *Freedom to Thrive: A Journey to Health*, is nearly complete. Find book release updates, speaking engagements, and coaching options at RootysRoots.com.

TRICIA SPEAS

Tricia Speas is well known for her compassion for others. That compassion led her to become a Certified Personal Empowerment Coach through Unstoppable Influence, and she was certified through John Maxwell. She is also certified as a Master Practitioner of NLP, Time Line Therapy™, and hypnosis.

She spent from 2012 to 2023 caregiving for the elderly, making sure they know they're important members of society and especially important to their families. She enjoys traveling. Her two sons and their families are her greatest pride and joy.

Throughout life, she has found that mentoring and coaching others comes naturally to her. Tricia is passionate about challenging her clients in their capabilities, inspiring them to be all they can, and to live to the fullest, no matter what stage in life they are at.

Tricia believes that life is a venture and commits to taking her client's hand, walking at their side, and encouraging them along the journey.

CHRISTINE L. STALLARD

Christine Stallard helps people rekindle their flame, master their mind, dare to dream, design a new path, and unleash their entrepreneurial spirit. In the process, they gain confidence and clarity to transition to an inspired life filled with passion and purpose, on their own terms and in any chapter.

Christine spent over 30 years in various government/ public affairs positions in the corporate world and as a consultant where she communicated and educated the general public and policymakers on electric utility and natural resource issues. She coached and mentored employees, coworkers, and friends to help them reach their personal and professional goals.

Christine is an entrepreneur, author, Personal Empowerment Coach, certified animal aromatherapist, avid college football fan (especially Penn State), quilter, and classical pianist. She lives in the Pacific Northwest with her husband and Bouvier des Flandres, Allium.

You can learn more about her at ChristineStallard.com.

ANNETTE STEIGER

Annette Steiger is a Certified Personal Empowerment Coach helping women who have experienced loss to overcome emptiness and fill their lives with more purpose and joy.

Annette has lived through grief and loss after being widowed in 2016. She has leaned into her lifelong relationship with God to lead her through this journey of healing and rediscovering who she is in this new season and to thrive after loss. Annette's passion is to help women heal from beliefs and wounds that have limited them so they can live in their full potential and authenticity and take up the charge to help heal the next generations.

Annette has three grown sons, three daughters-in-law, and three granddaughters. She retired after a career as a Senior Project Manager and Certified Project Management Professional. She holds a Master of Science in Instructional Design and Human Performance Technology with a bachelor's degree in Computer Information Systems.

BECKY WALLERY

Becky Wallery is on a mission to help others figure out who they truly are so they can take back their life. As a Transformation and Mindset Coach, Becky works to empower her clients to recognize they have more choices in how to live their dream life.

In her previous role as a Senior Software Development Manager, she managed worldwide teams and coached team members. She loves walking alongside others in their personal and professional adventures.

In 2016, she had what she calls her "awakening," which helped her to realize that she was meant for something more in her life. This led her to join a network marketing company, where she started her personal journey to take back her life.

Her personal motto became "Dream Bigger; Believe Deeply; Live Intentionally."

Taking back her life resulted in her becoming a Personal Empowerment Coach.

She also uses NLP, TimeLine Therapy, and Hypnosis to help unlock limiting beliefs buried in the subconscious mind. Becky is also an inspirational speaker.

She founded Uplift Your Soul with a mission to uplift others and bring more love and peace to the lives of her customers.

Becky lives in Boise, Idaho, with her husband, Michael, and their three amazing children. They enjoy camping, riding ATVs and spending time outside as a family.

ELLIE WEST

Ellie West is a purser flight attendant for a major airline and has had the privilege to serve others utilizing her gifts in hospitality for over 40 years. She is a Certified Personal Empowerment Coach and Certified Master Practitioner and Coach of NLP, Time Line Therapy, and Hypnosis.

With a heart for connecting with others, Ellie has been recognized in the top 1% of flight attendants, Chairman's Club Honoree, and the recipient of the Go-Giver Award from Unstoppable Influence. She writes weekly articles that bring positivity, inspiration, and encouragement to her local communities.

Ellie desires to empower others to create fulfilling careers and a life they love. She helps them discover their purpose and potential by uncovering their limiting beliefs.

Ellie and her husband, Bill, live in her native state of Montana.

Social media: @coachelliewest

Email: coachingbyellie@gmail.com

Website: CoachingHeartToHeart.com

REFERENCES

Angelou, Maya. 1978. *And Still I Rise*. New York: Random House.

Angelou, Maya. 2001. *Life Mosaic*. Kansas City, MO: Hallmark.

Angelou, Maya. 2009. *Letter to My Daughter*. New York: Random House Trade Paperbacks.

Bond, Beverly, ed. 2018. *Black Girls Rock!: Owning Our Magic. Rocking Our Truth*. New York: 37 INK.

Caligiuri, Ross. 2017. *Dreaming in the Shadows*. Phoenix, AZ: Ross Caligiuri.

Coelho, Paulo. 2018. "Maybe the journey isn't so much about becoming someone. Maybe it's about getting rid of everything that isn't really you. #HIPPIE." Twitter, June 24, 2018. https://twitter.com/paulocoelho/status/1010864837784690689.a

Curie, Eve. (1937) 2001. *Madame Curie: A Biography*. New York: Hachette Books.

Eldredge, John. 2016. *Walking with God*. Nashville, TN: Nelson Books.

Gallup. 2023. "CliftonStrengths." https://www.gallup.com/cliftonstrengths/en/254033/strengthsfinder.aspx.

Greven, Corina, U., Francesca Lionetti, Charlotte Booth, Elaine N. Aron, Elaine Fox, Haline E. Schendan, Michael Pluess, Hilgo Bruining, Bianca Acevedo, Patricia Bijttebier, and Judith Homberg. 2019. "Sensory Processing Sensitivity in the Context of Environmental Sensitivity: A Critical Review and Development of Research Agenda." Neuroscience & Biobehavioral Reviews 98: 287–305. doi.org/10.1016/j.neubiorev.2019.01.009.

Grey, R. S. 2014. *Scoring Wilder*. Scotts Valley, CA: CreateSpace Publishing.

Guo, Kristina L. 2008. " DECIDE: A Decision-Making Model for More Effective Decision Making by Health Care Managers." *The Health Care Manager* 27 (2): 118–127. https://journals.lww.com/health-caremanagerjournal/Abstract/2008/04000/DE-CIDE__A_Decision_Making_Model_for_More_Effective.5.aspx.a

Hazlett, Natasha. 2018. *Unstoppable Influence: Be You. Be Fearless. Transform Lives.* Boise, ID: Soul Food Publishing.

Hill, Napoleon. (1937) 2005. *Think and Grow Rich*. Reprint, New York: Penguin Group.

Keys, Alicia. 2014. "I pledge to Ban Bossy and encourage girls to lead. Join me at http://banbossy.com/ to take the pledge and get leadership tips for girls. Feeling this! #banbossy." Facebook, March

10, 2014. https://www.facebook.com/aliciakeys/photos/i-pledge-to-ban-bossy-and-encourage-girls-to-lead-join-me-at-httpbanbossycom-to-/10151937150927051/.

Leaf, Caroline. 2018–2023. *Cleaning up the Mental Mess.* Podcast. https://drleaf.com/pages/podcasts.

Maté, Gabor. 2019. "Authenticity vs. Attachment." CRAZYWISE. May 14, 2019. YouTube video, 4:18. https://youtu.be/l3bynimi8HQ.

Meyer, Joyce. 2023. "Get Out of That Pit!" Joyce Meyer Ministries. https://joycemeyer.org/everydayanswers/ea-teachings/Get-Out-of-That-Pit.

Orloff, Judith. 2017. *The Empath's Survival Guide: Life Strategies for Sensitive People.* Boulder, CO: Sounds True.

Parade. 2008. "'Family Is All We Have In Life." *Parade,* November 23, 2008. https://parade.com/49840/parade/family-is-all-we-have-in-life/.

Ramis, Harold, dir. 1993. *Groundhog Day.* Culver City, CA: Columbia Pictures.

Seuss, Dr. 1959. *Happy Birthday to You!* New York: Random House Children's Books.

Sollisch, Jim. 2016. "The Cure for Decision Fatigue." *Wall Street Journal,* June 10, 2016. https://www.wsj.com/articles/the-cure-for-decision-fatigue-1465596928.

The Bible, 2 Corinthians 10:5 (NIV).

The Bible, Isaiah 26:3–4 (NLT).

The Bible, Isaiah 62:3.

The Bible, John 8:32.

The Bible, Matthew 25:14–30.

The Bible, Matthew 5:14–15 (KJV) .

The Bible, Psalm 139:13–14 (ESV).

The Bible, Psalm 25:4.

The Bible, Psalm 139:13–14.

The Bible, Psalm 139:18 (TPT).

The Bible, Psalm 23:4 (TPT).

Williamson, Marianne. 1996. *A Return to Love.* New York: Harper Perennial.

Winfrey, Oprah. "Oprah: Heed to the Whispers of the Universe." Oprah.com. https://www.oprah.com/own-digitaloriginals/oprah-pay-attention-to-the-whispers-of-the-universe-video.

Youn, Soo. 2015. "Nicole Kidman: 'I Was Afraid of My Own Power'." *The Cut,* June 17, 2015. https://www.thecut.com/2015/06/nicole-kidman-i-was-afraid-of-my-own-power.html.

Made in the USA
Columbia, SC
09 February 2025

53300064R00190